PIANO MARVEL METHOD • LEVEL 1

C0-BLC-601

pianomarvel

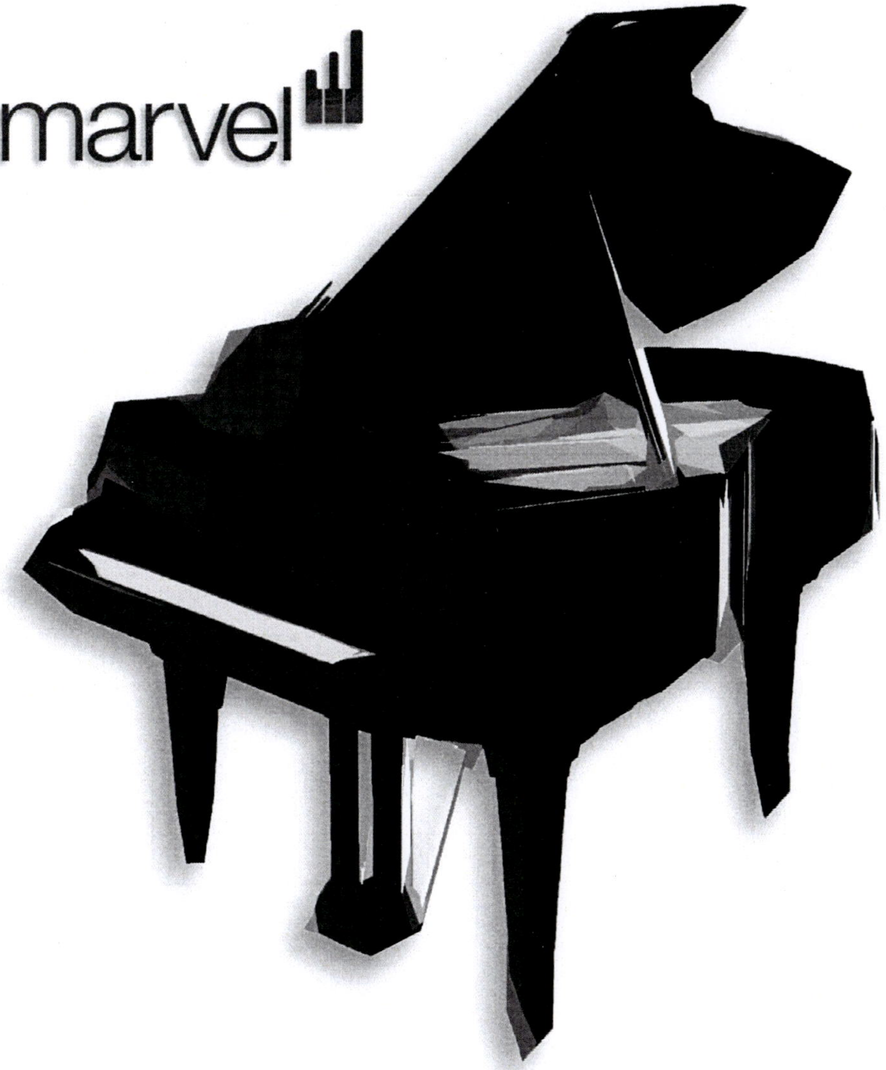

by Aaron G. Garner

Piano Marvel LLC 2011

Table of Contents

Page		
4	Introduction to the Grand Staff and the Keyboard	
5	Posture and Finger Numbers	

Page	Method 1A	Score	Date
6	Whole Notes & Whole Rests		
7	Half Notes & Half Rests		
8	Quarter Notes		
9	C Song		
10	Not the C Song		
11	Whole Notes (R&L) (Switching Hands)		
12	Half Notes (R&L)		
13	Quarter Notes (R&L)		
14	Quarter Notes (R&L) No. 2		
15	C Song (R&L)		
16	C Song (Two Hands)		
17	Copycat (Listen & Repeat)		
18	Copycat		
19	Eighth Notes		
20	C Song Eighth Notes		
21	1A Review		

Page	Method 1B	Score	Date
22	D Song		
23	CDC Song		
24	B Song		
25	CBC Song		
26	CB Song		
27	DBD Song		
28	DCD Song		
29	Hot Cross Buns		
30	Merrily We Roll Along		
31	Jazz		
32	Fandango		
33	Middle Landian CDE		
34	Agent ABC		
35	1B Review		

PIANO MARVEL

© 2011 All Rights Reserved

Page	Method 1C		Score	Date
36	Peter Peter			
38	Ice Man			
39	Sands of Time			
40	Ten Little Indian Rhythm			
41	Get Off the Tracks			
42	Indians			
43	1C Review			

Page	Method 1D		Score	Date
44	Quiet Moments (RH)	F		
45	Never Never Land			
46	Walk Down to G	G		
47	Texas			
48	Mother May I?	*f*		
49	Daytime	*p*		
50	Jolly Old Saint Nicholas			
51	Yankee Doodle			
52	The Dotted Half Note	𝅗𝅥.		
53	The Dotted Quarter Note	♩.		
54	Lion Soup			
55	Solemn Reflections			
56	1D Review			

Page	Method 1E	Score	Date
58	Jupiter (Introduction to G)		
59	Saturn		
60	Uranus		
61	Neptune		
62	Earth		
63	Pirates		
64	Flowing (Introduction to F)		
65	Waters		
66	Trickle		
67	Endlessly		
68	Away		
69	Camptown Races		
70	Old MacDonald		
72	1E Review		

Page	Tests	Score	Date
73	Note Value Test		
74	Terms & Signs Test		
75	Grand Staff Test		
76	Note Test		

© 2011 All Rights Reserved

Introduction to the Grand Staff and the Keyboard

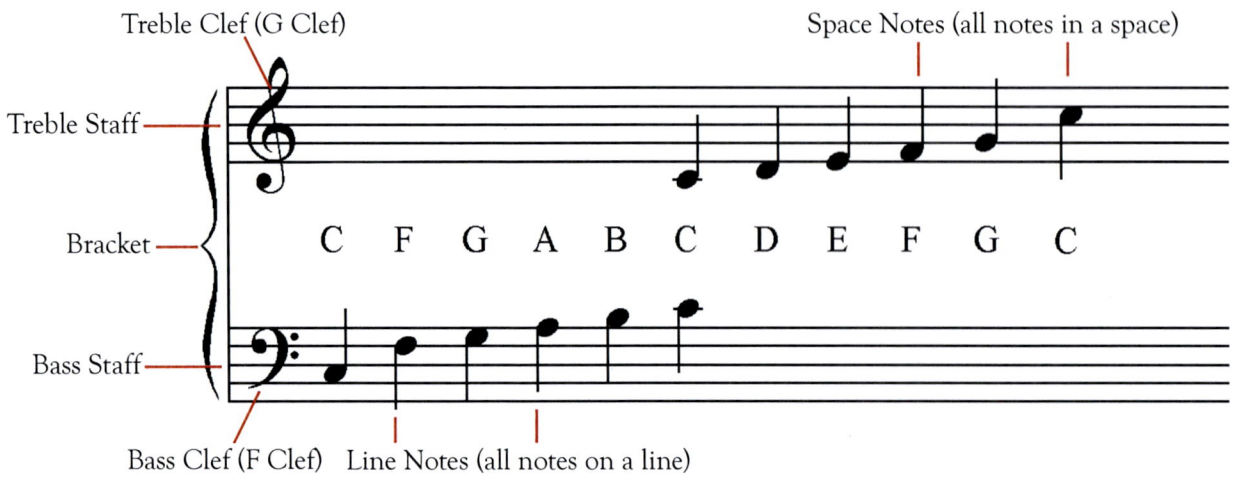

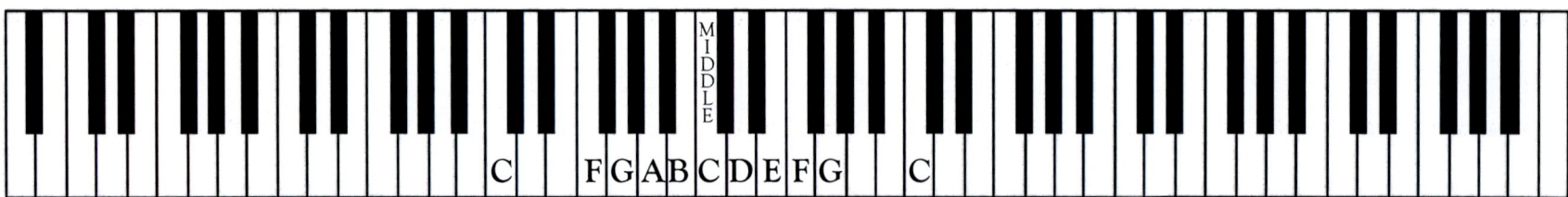

Posture and Finger Numbers

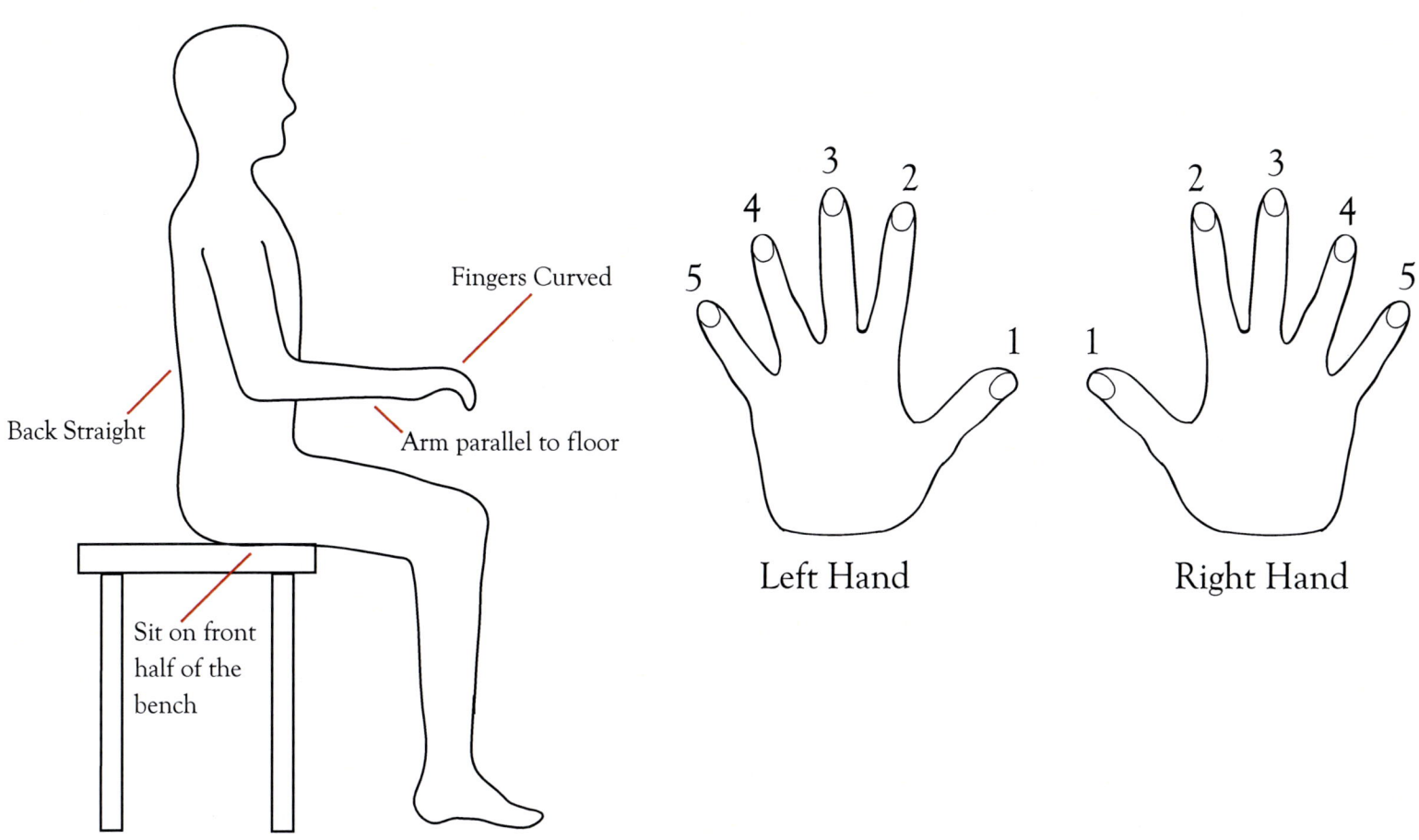

1A

○ Hold 4 counts
▬ Rest 4 counts

Whole Notes & Whole Rests
Middle C

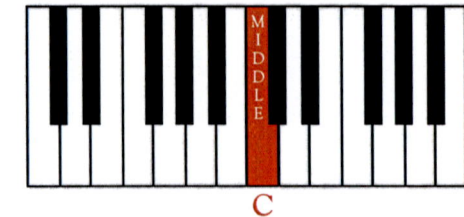
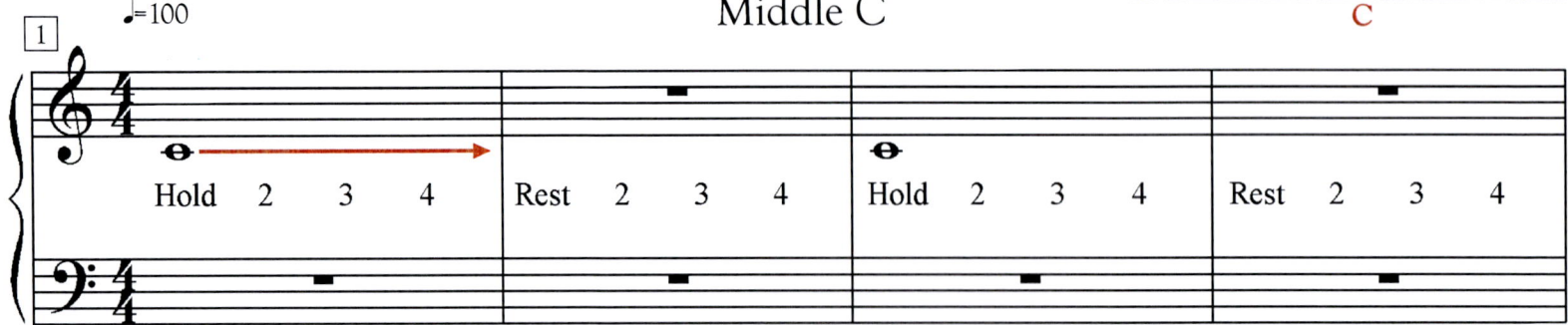
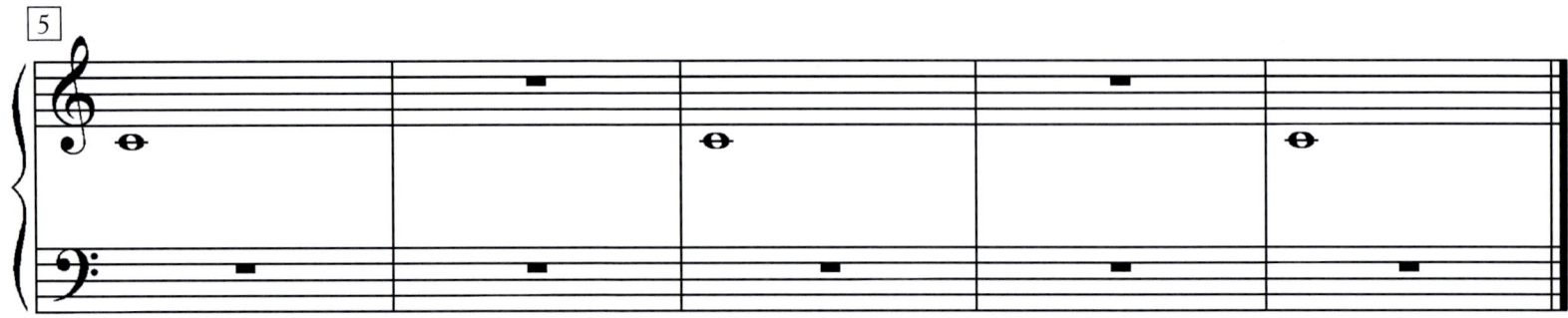

*Student plays 8va

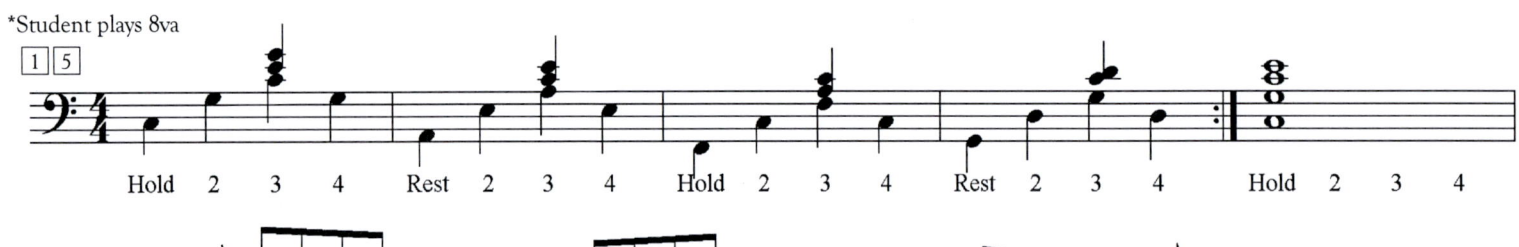

Alternate Accompaniment

Half Notes & Half Rests

Hold 2 counts
Rest 2 counts

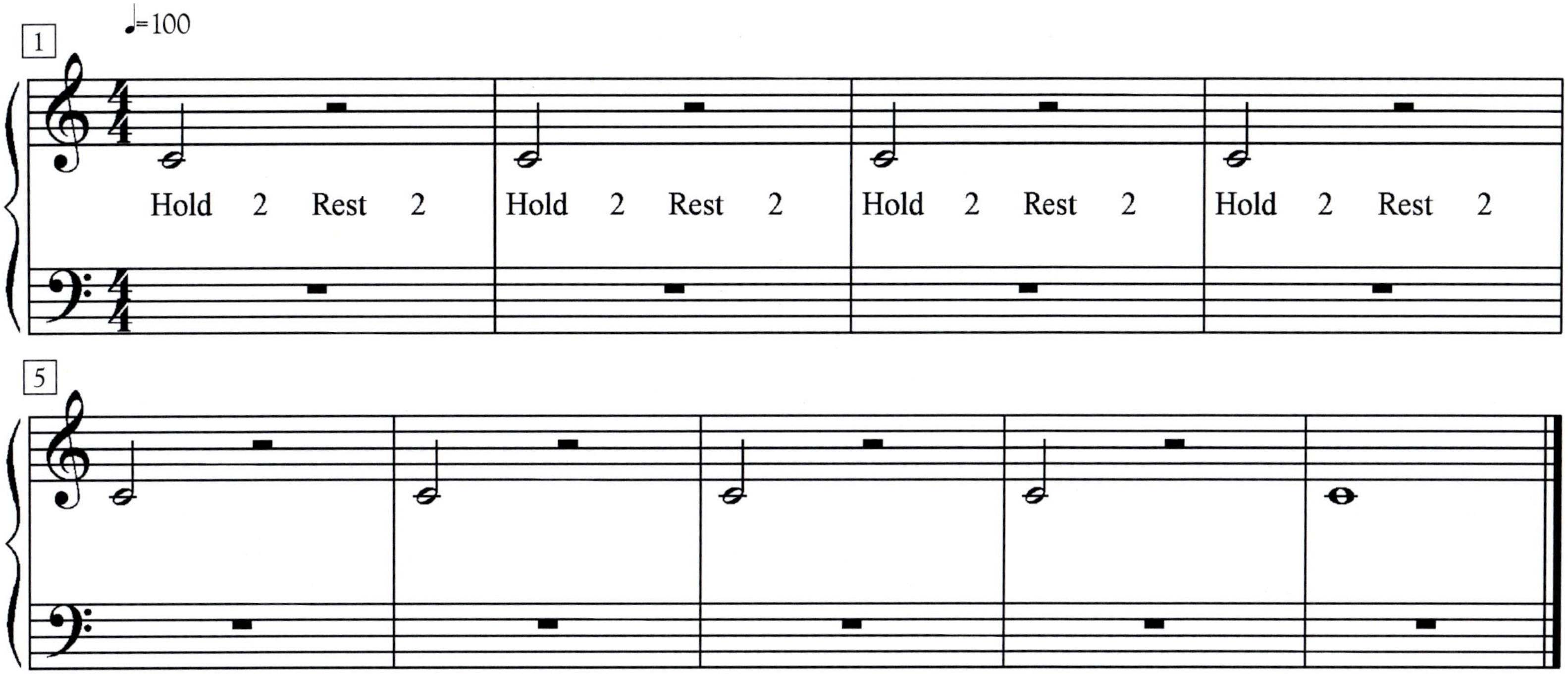

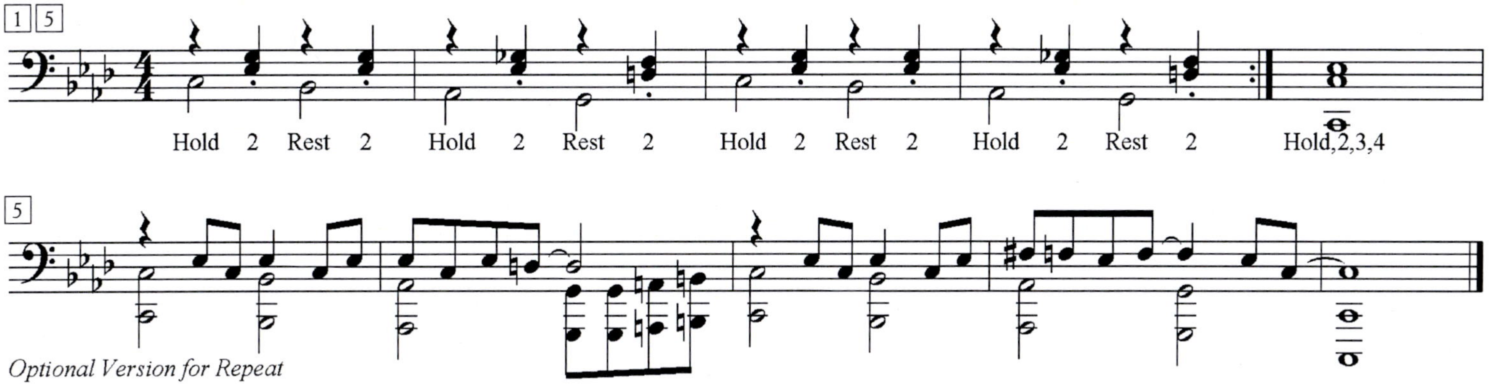

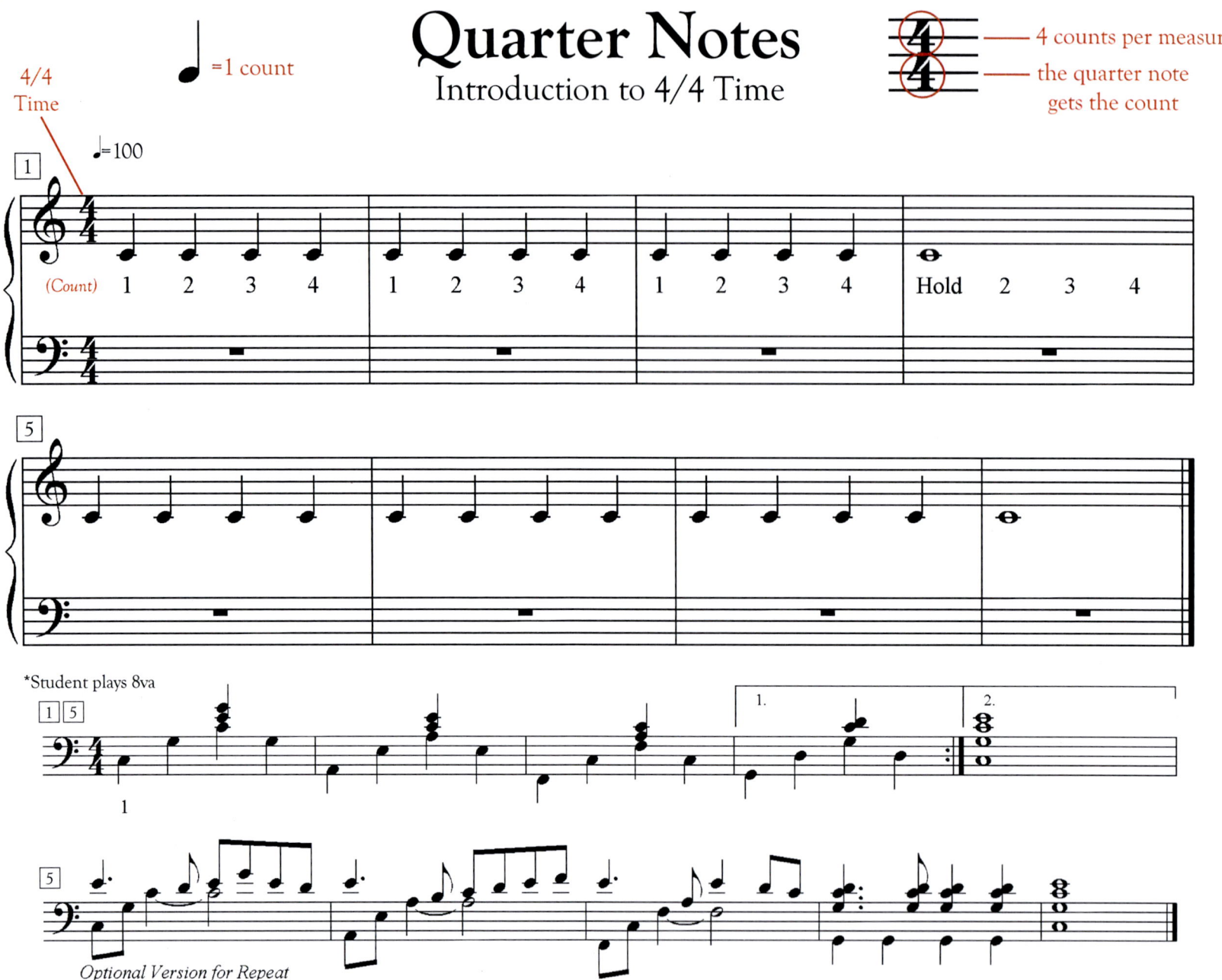

C Song

1. Clap and count out loud
2. Write the counts (2nd line)

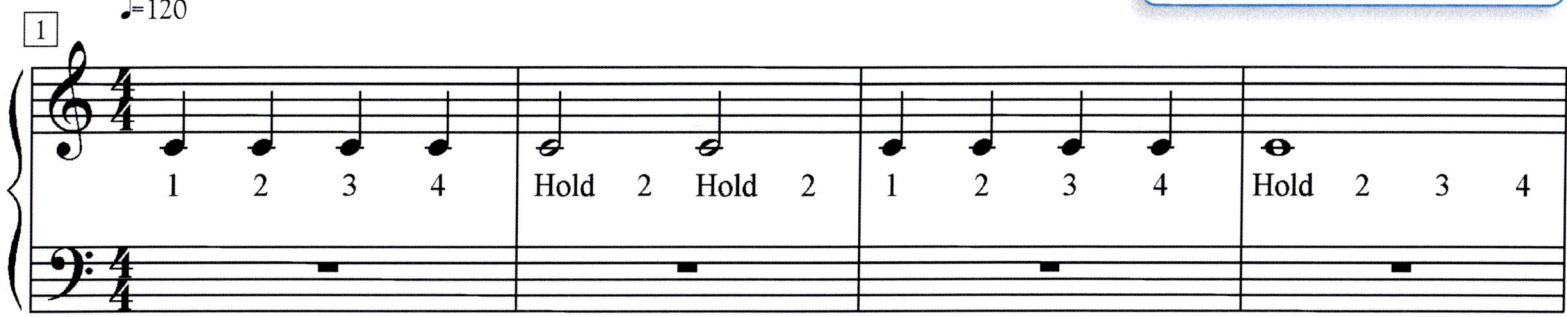

*Student plays 8va

Not the C Song

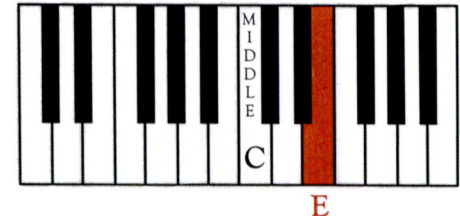

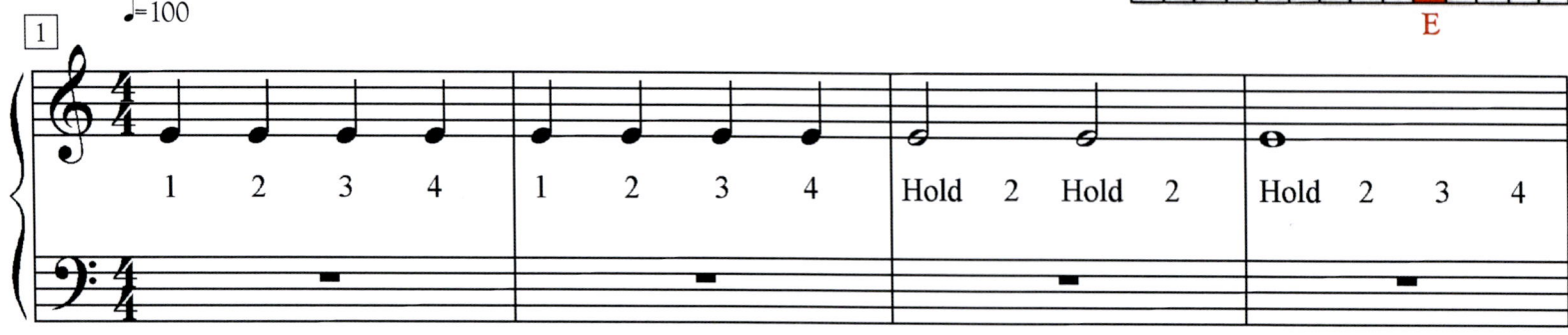

*Student plays 8va

Optional Version for Repeat

Whole Notes (R&L)
Switching Hands

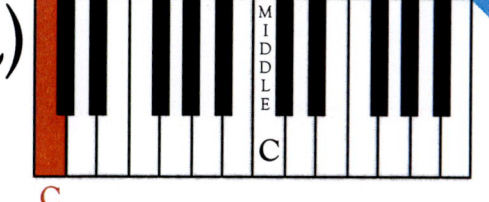

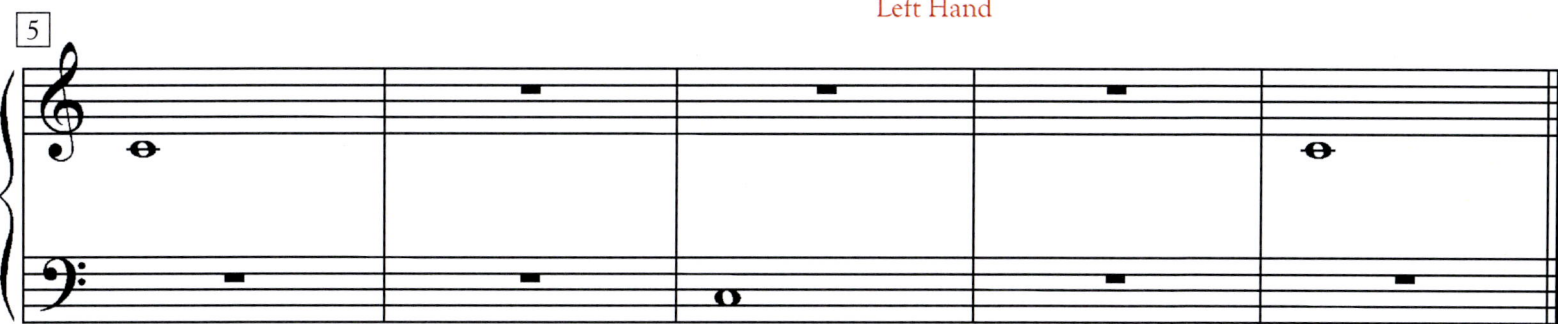

*Student plays 15ma

Half Notes (R&L)

Quarter Notes (R&L)

C Song (R&L)

*Student plays 15ma

C Song (Two Hands)

Copycat
Listen & Repeat

Student copies the teacher
1. Clap
2. Clap and count
3. Play and count

1A

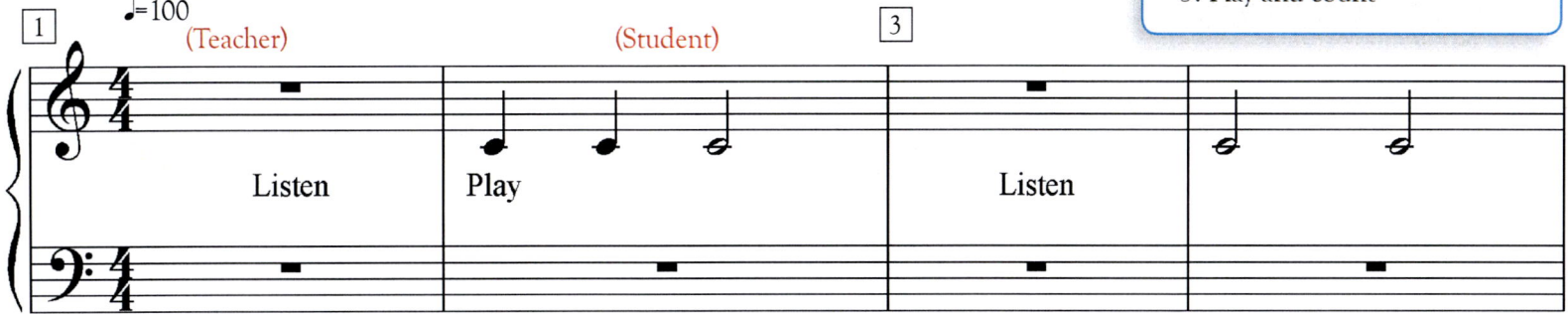

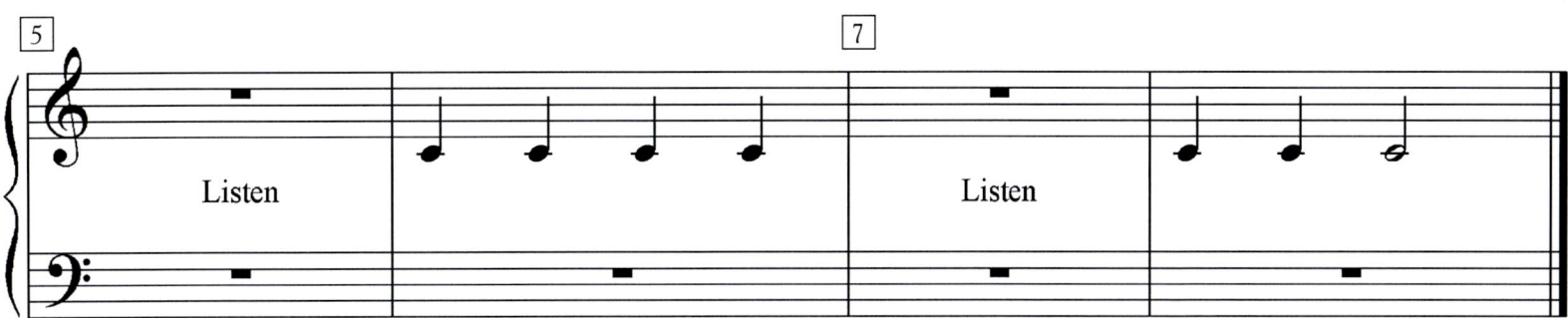

*Student plays 8va

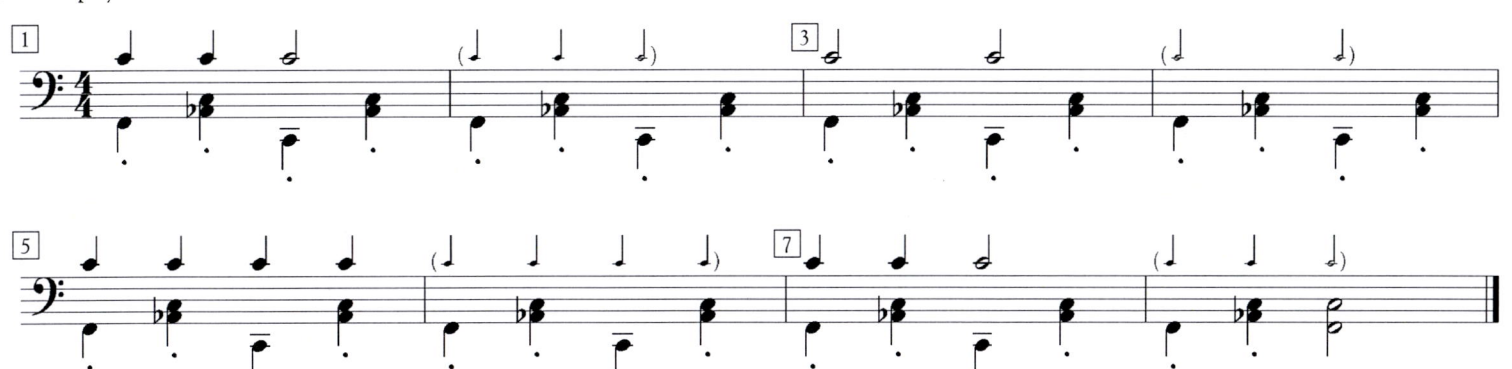

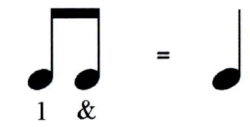

Copycat
Introduction to Eighth Notes

2 Eighth Notes = 1 count

Student copies the teacher
1. Clap
2. Clap and count
3. Play and count

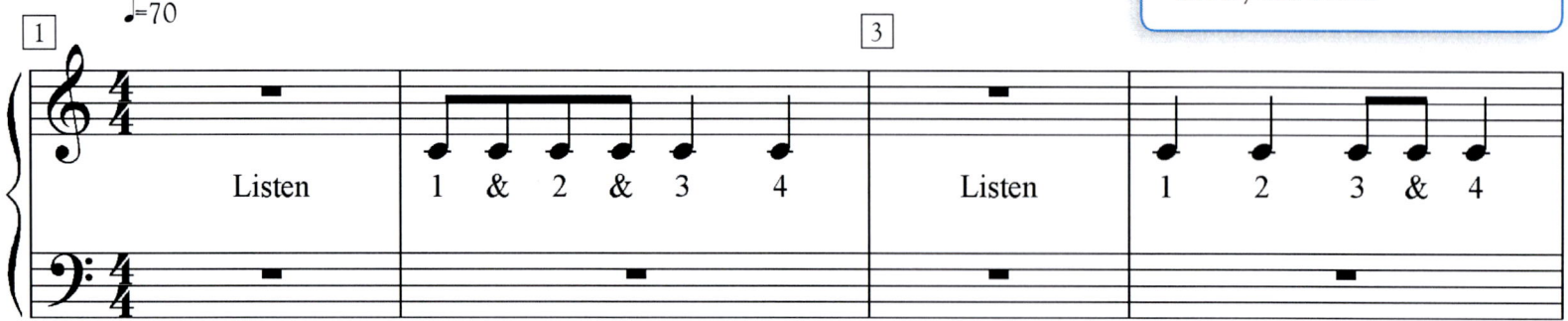

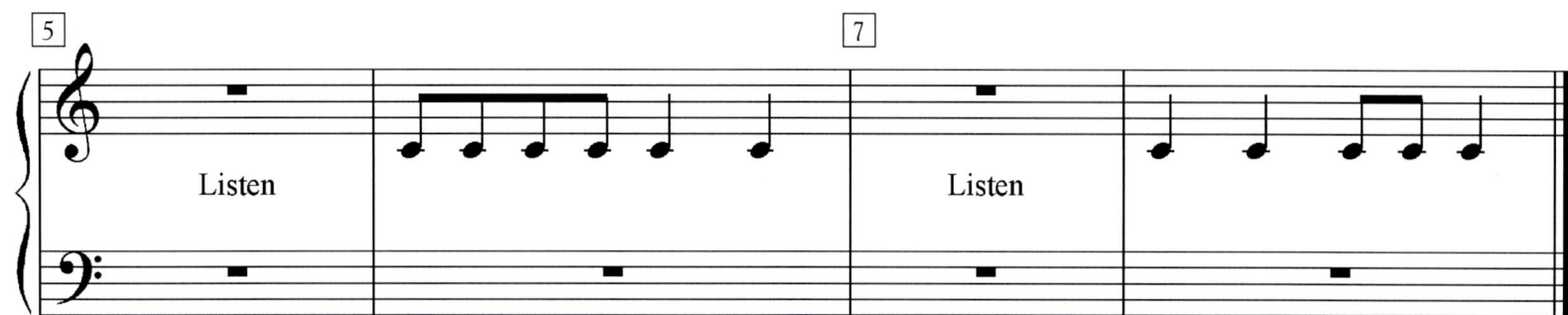

*Student plays 8va

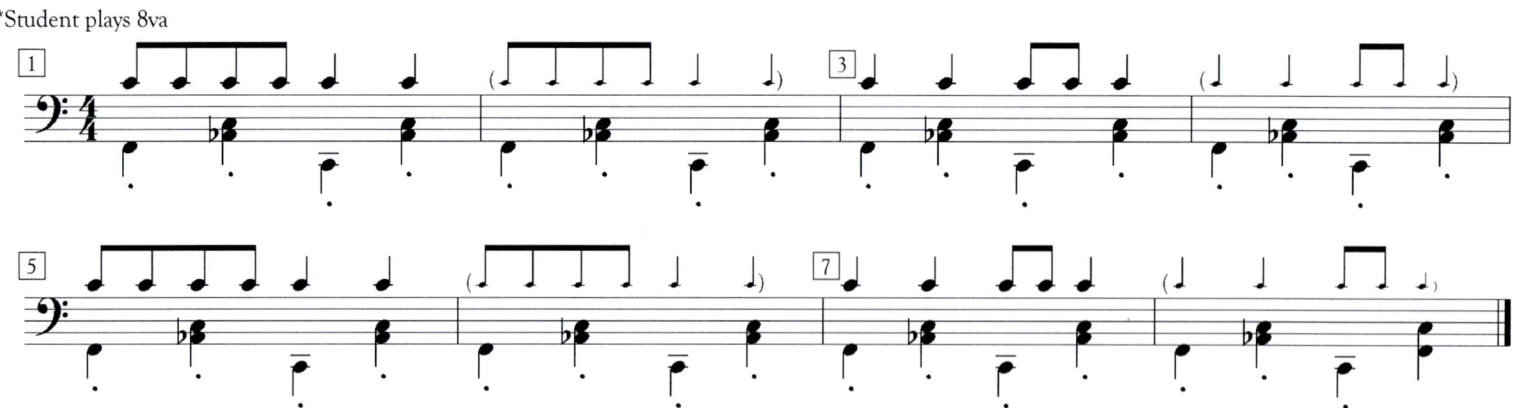

Eighth Notes
Count Out Loud

1. Clap and count
2. Play and count

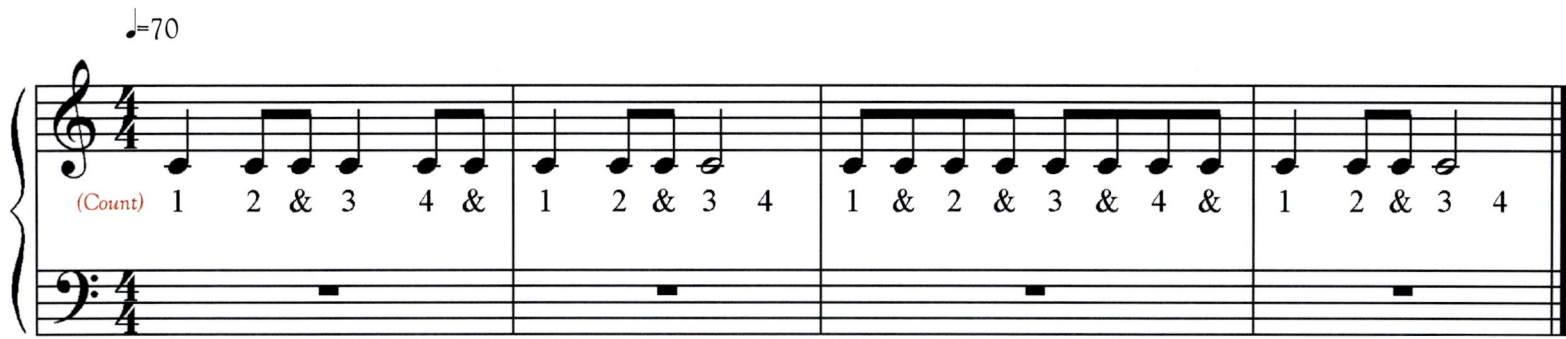

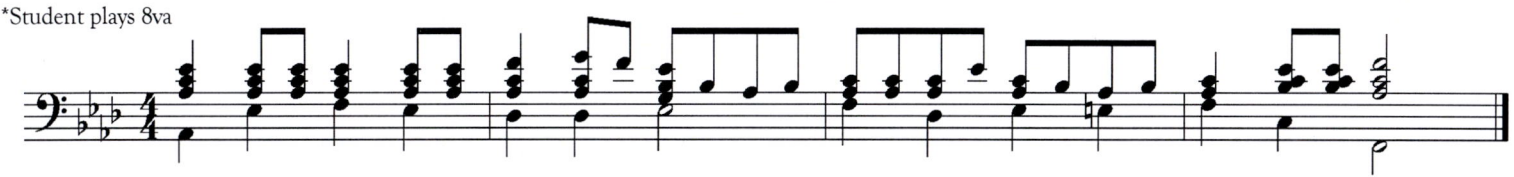

*Student plays 8va

C Song Eighth Notes

1A Review

1. Match the symbol with the correct definition.

1. ➖ _____ Half Note (2 beats)

2. 𝄞 _____ 4/4 Time

3. ♩ _____ Bass Clef (Left Hand)

4. 𝄢 _____ Quarter Rest

5. 𝅝 _____ Double Eighth Notes

6. 4/4 _____ Half Rest

7. ▬ _____ Whole Note (4 Beats)

8. 𝅗𝅥 _____ Quarter Note (1 Beat)

9. 𝄽 _____ Whole Rest

10. ♫ _____ Treble Clef (Right Hand)

2. Visit pianomarvel.com and take the Standard Assessment of Sight Reading, then record your score.

SASR Score

3. Choose and learn a piece from the online Piano Marvel library.

© 2011   All Rights Reserved

1B

D Song
Introduction to D

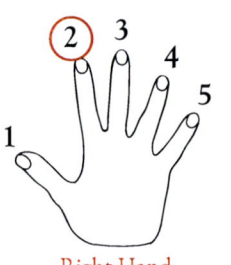
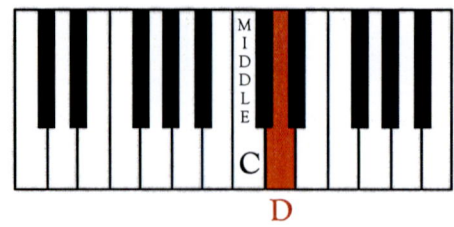
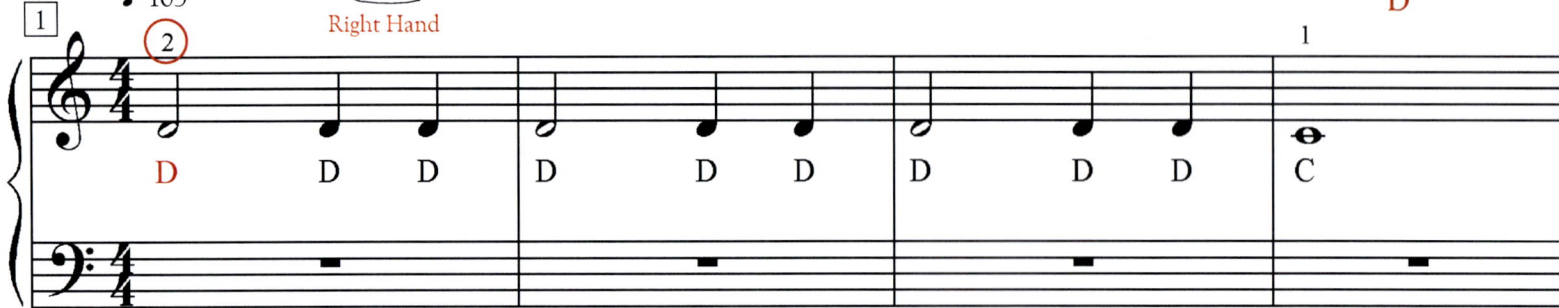

*Student plays 8va

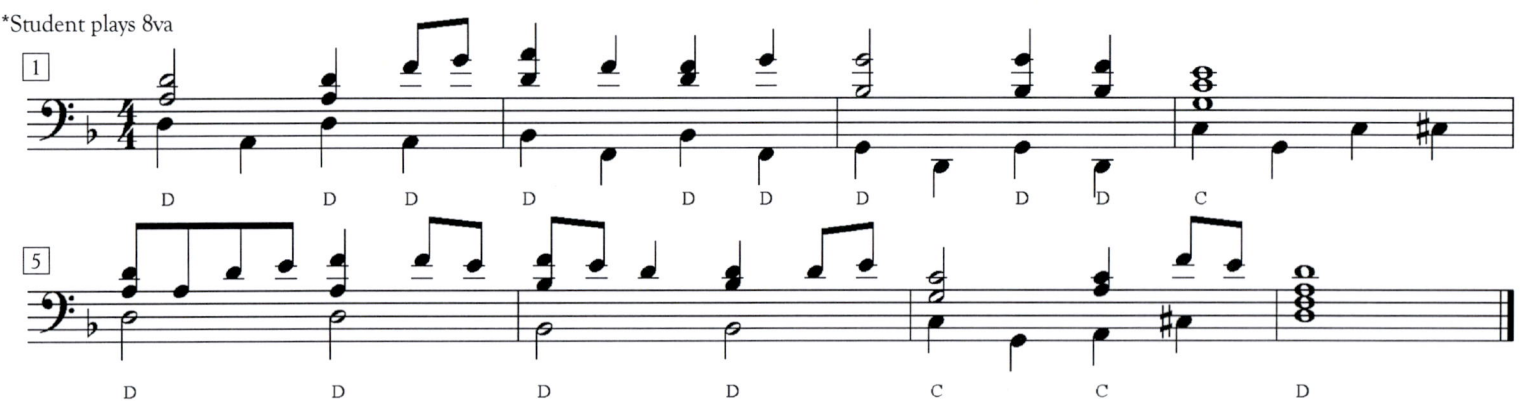

CDC Song

1. Clap and count out loud
2. Write note names (2nd line)

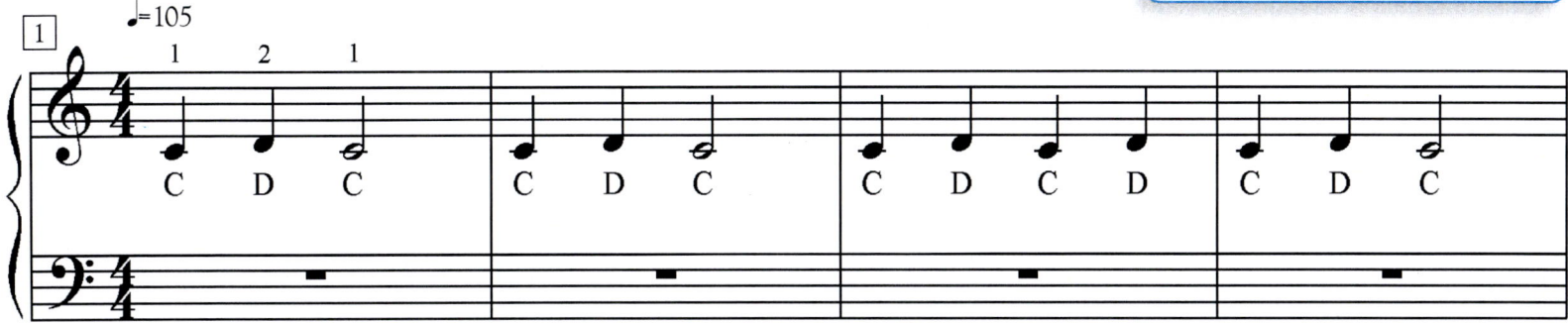

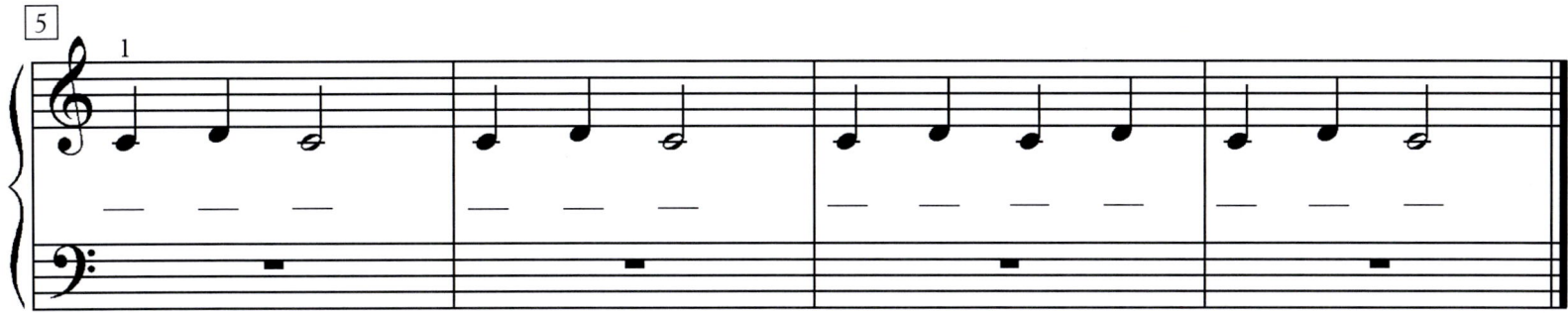

*Student plays 8va

Swing

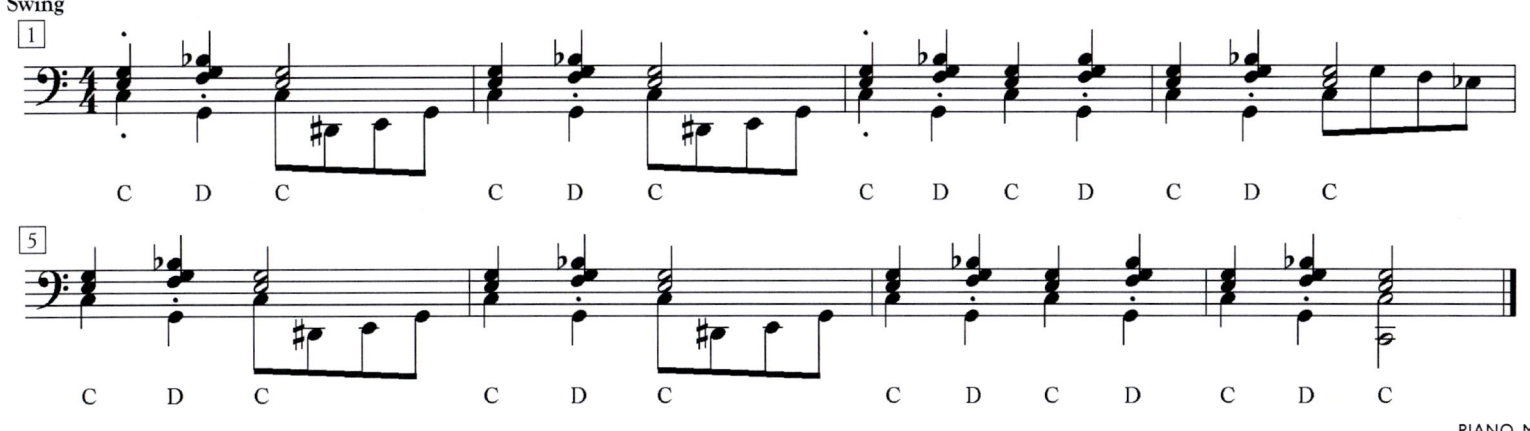

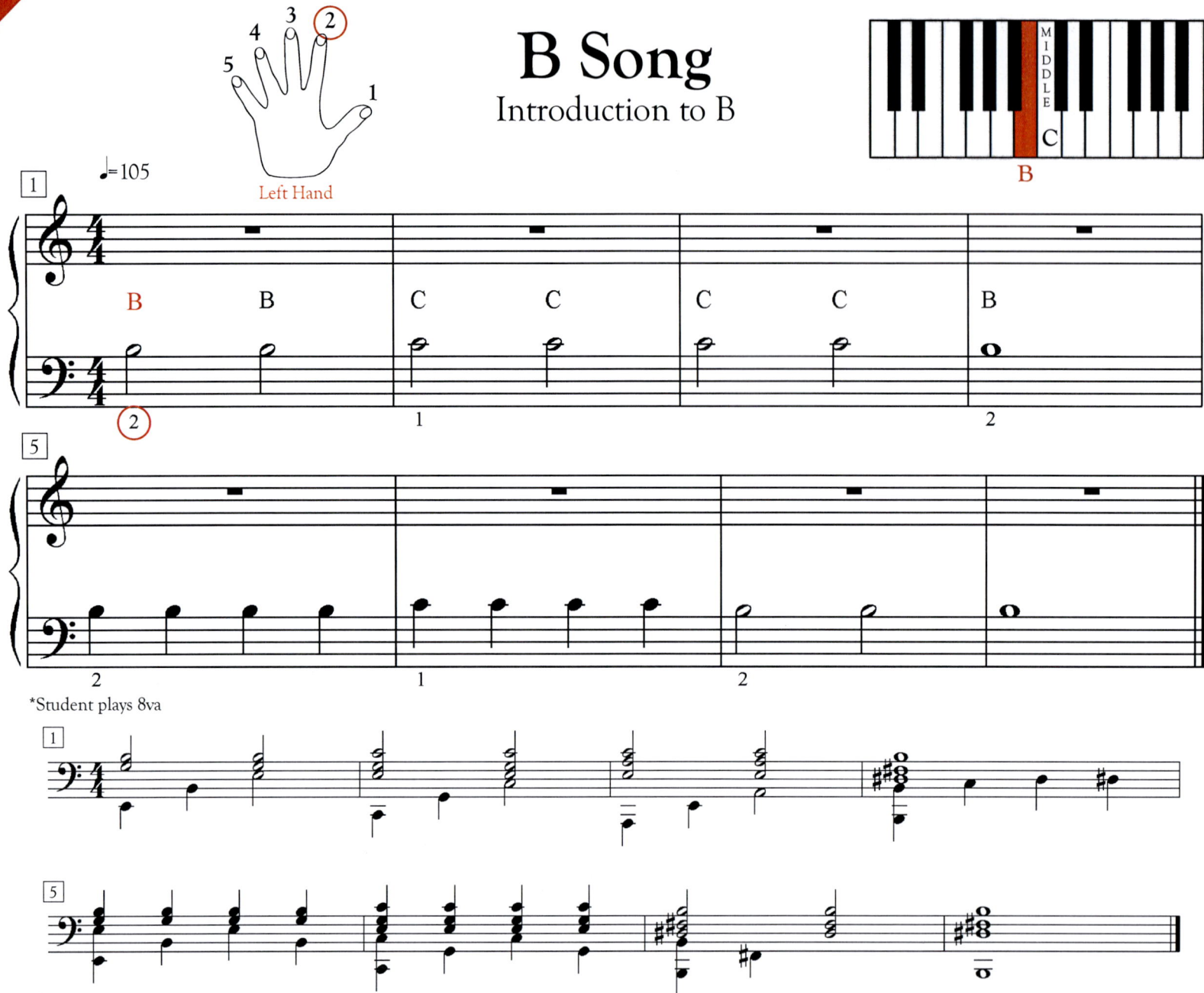

CBC Song

1. Clap and count out loud
2. Write note names (2nd line)

CB Song
Introducing the Repeat Sign

Repeat sign means to start over from the beginning

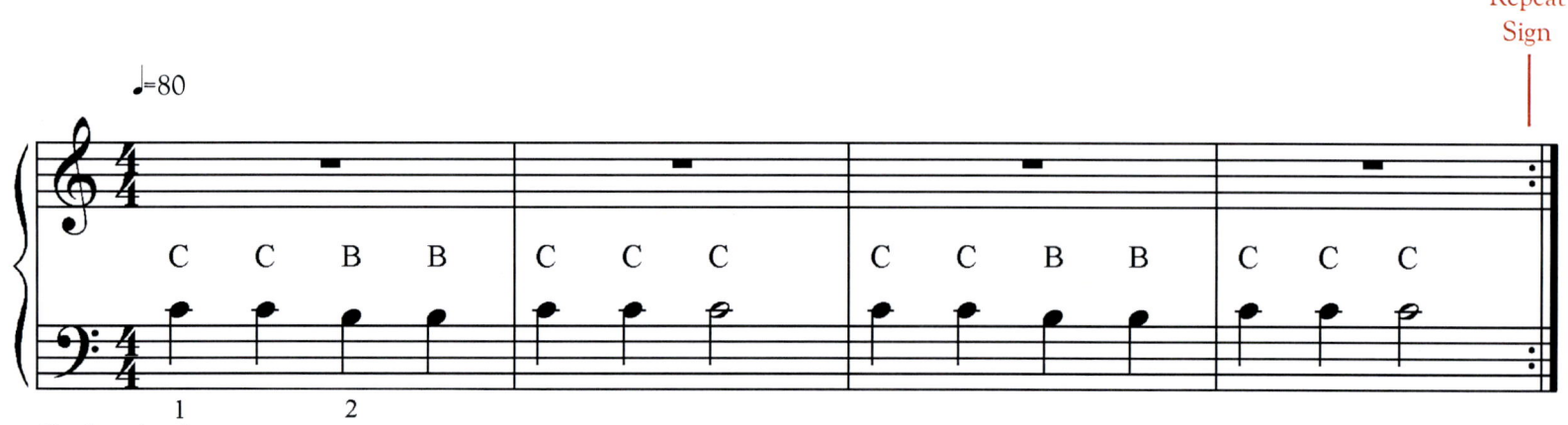

DBD Song

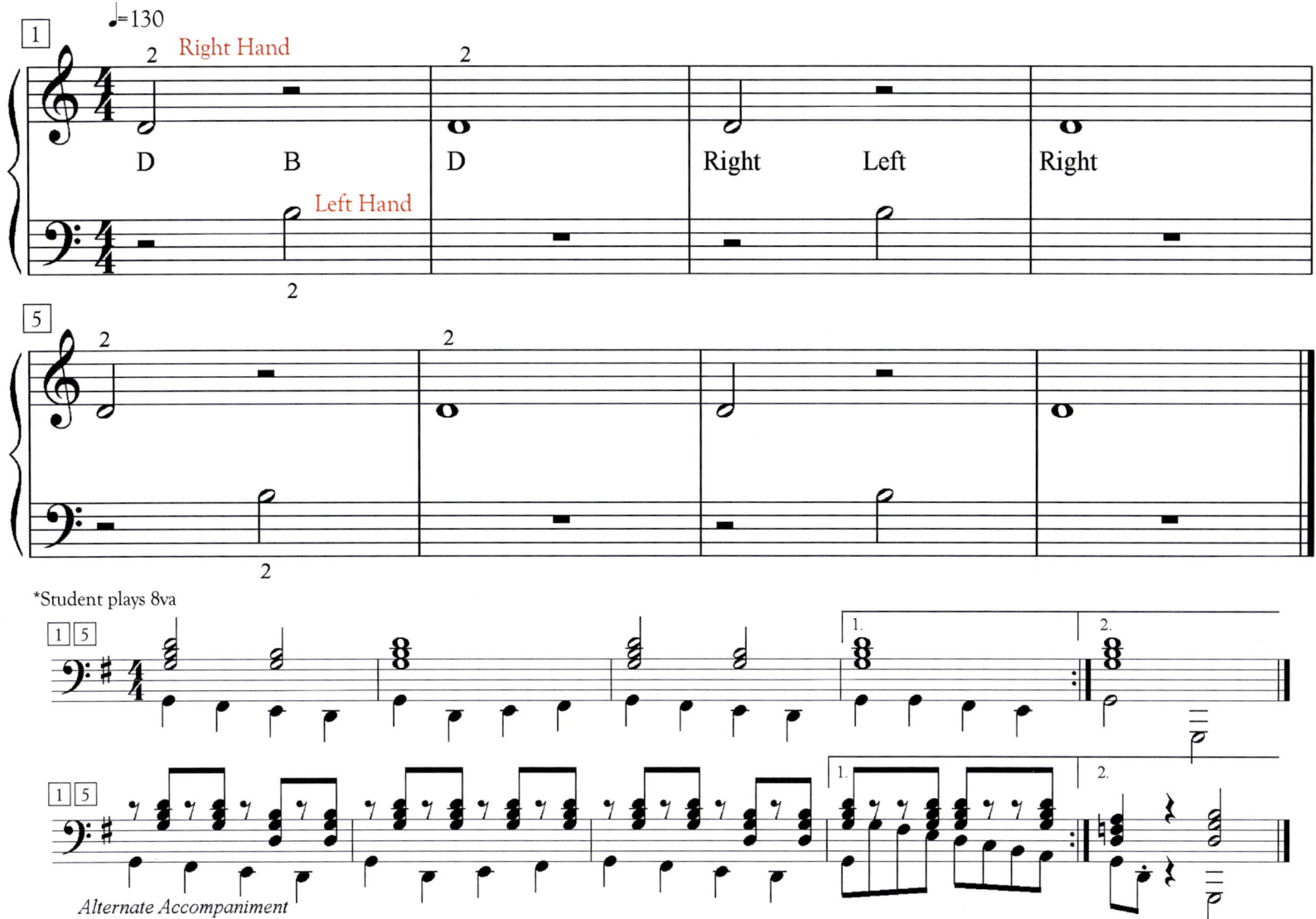

DCD Song

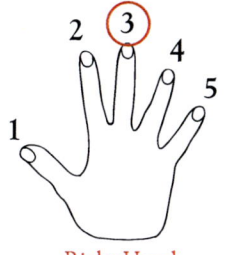

Hot Cross Buns
Introduction to E

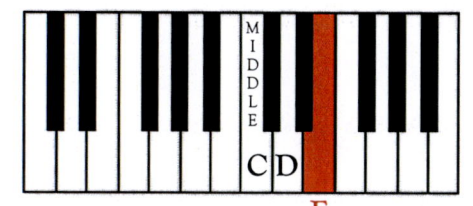

Traditional

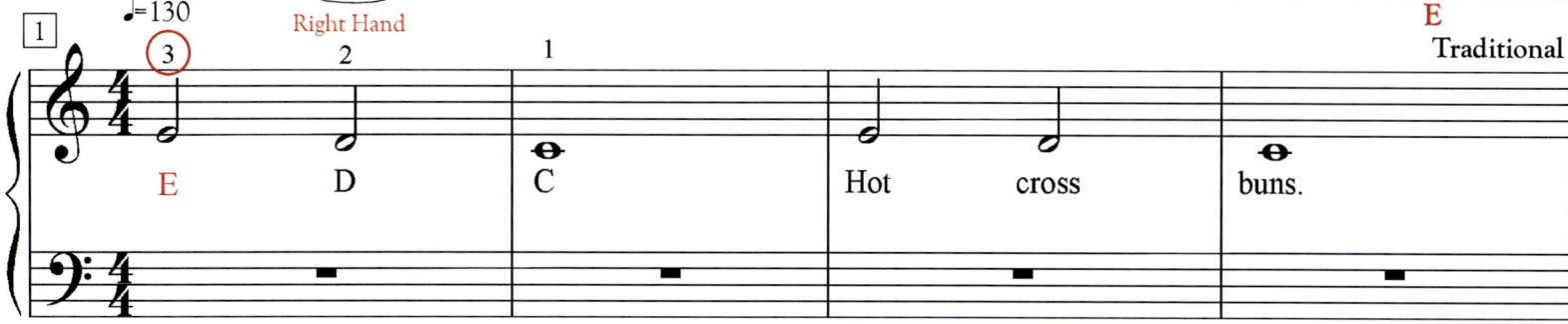

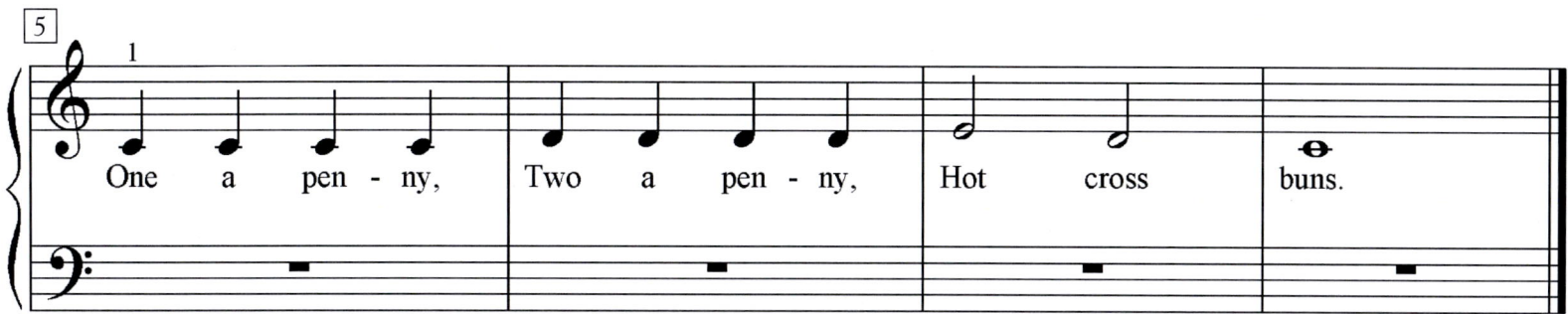

*Student plays 8va

Merrily We Roll Along

Traditional

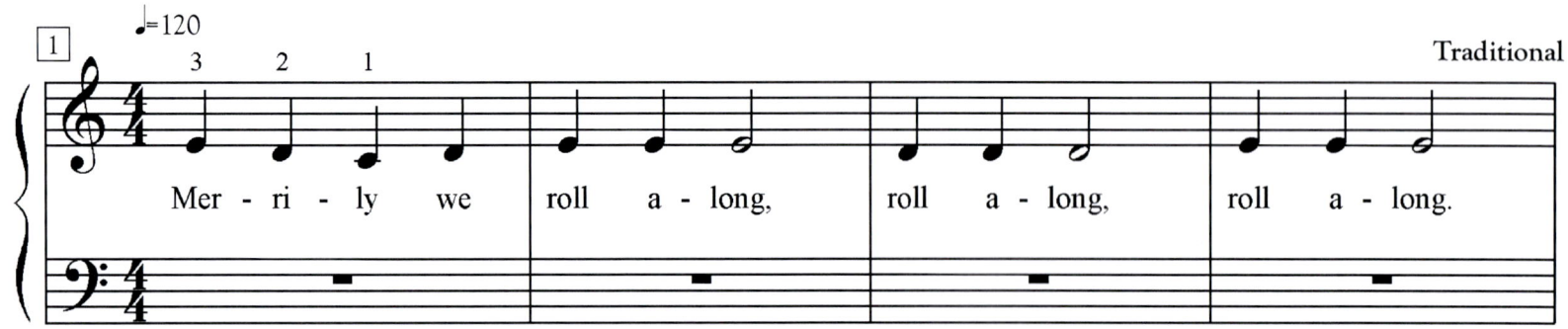

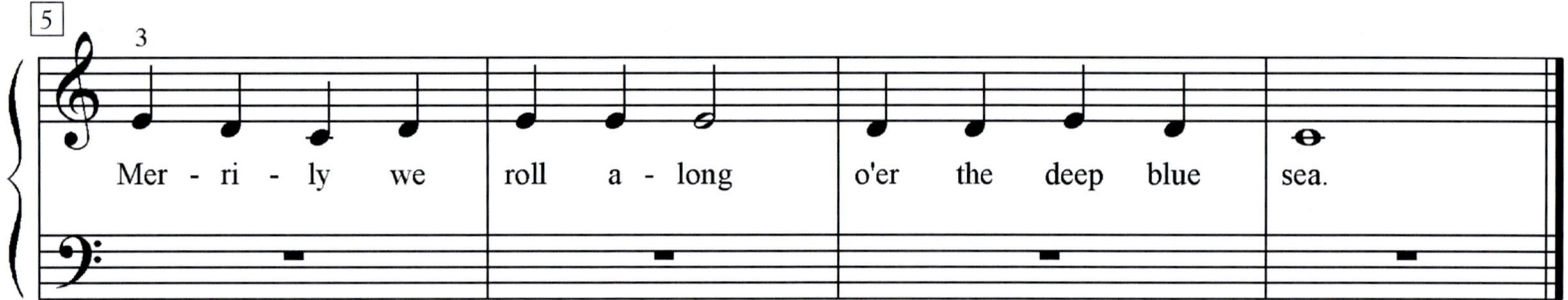

*Student plays 8va

Alternate Accompaniment

Fandango

Introduction to 6/8 Time

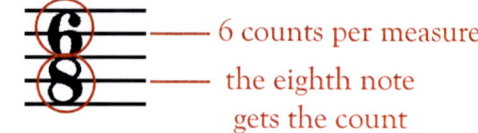

6 counts per measure
the eighth note gets the count

Aaron Garner

6/8 Time
♩.=120
1
1 2 3 4 5 6
1 2 3 4 5 6
1 2 3 4 5 6
B
1
2
3
2
5
1
2
3

*Student plays 8va

1
5

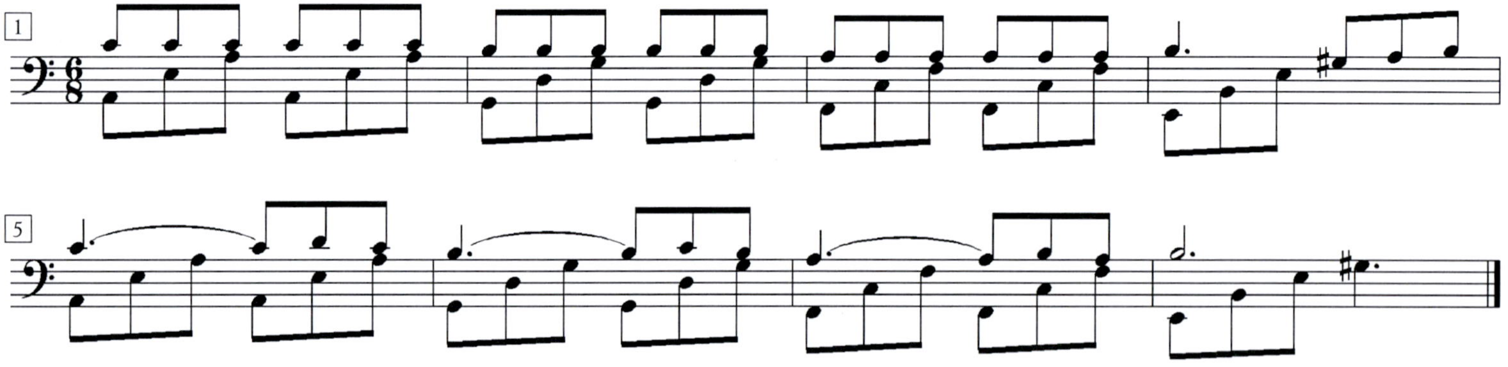

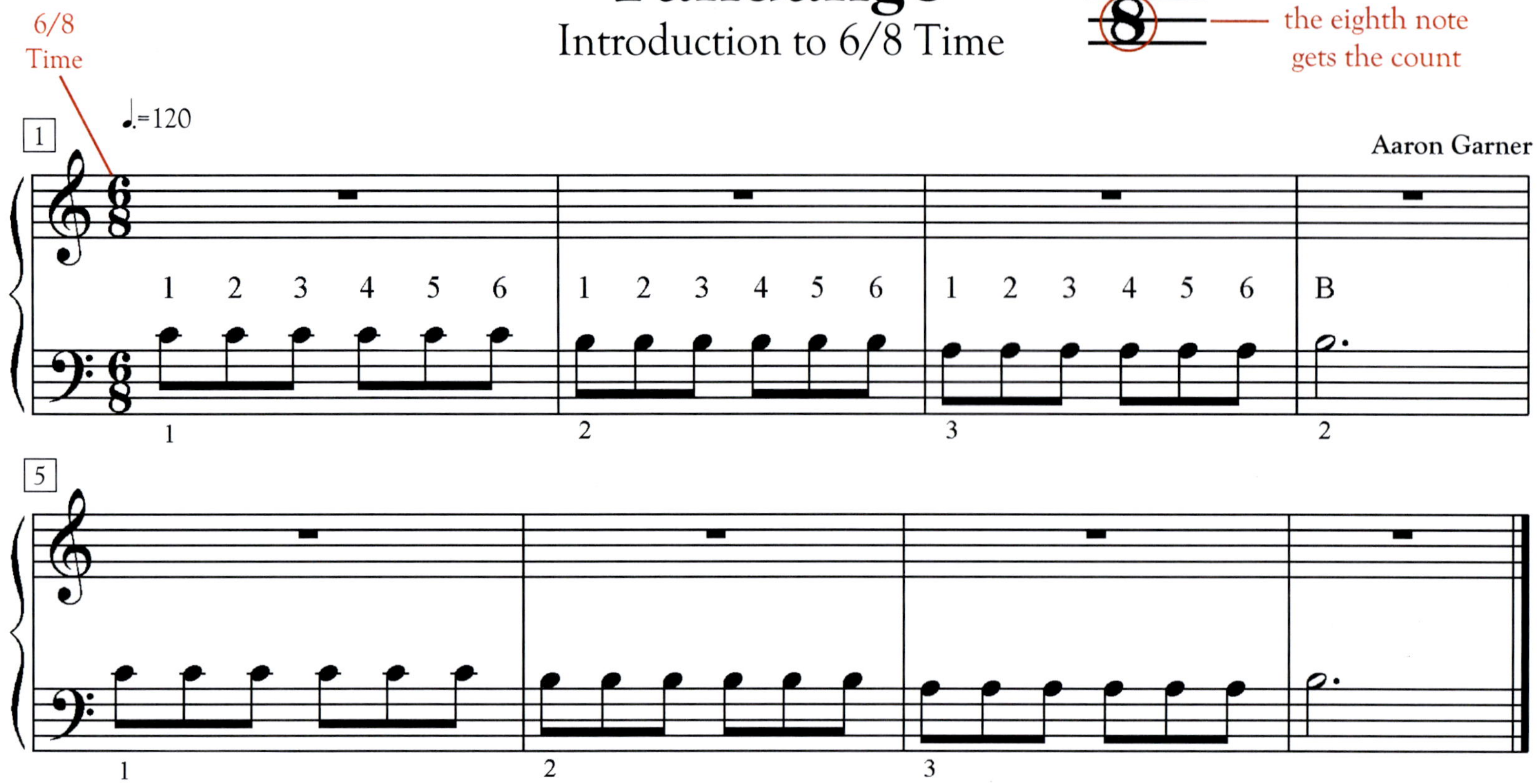

Middle Landian CDE

1B

Write note names (2nd line)

♩=120

Aaron Garner

E C E D C D

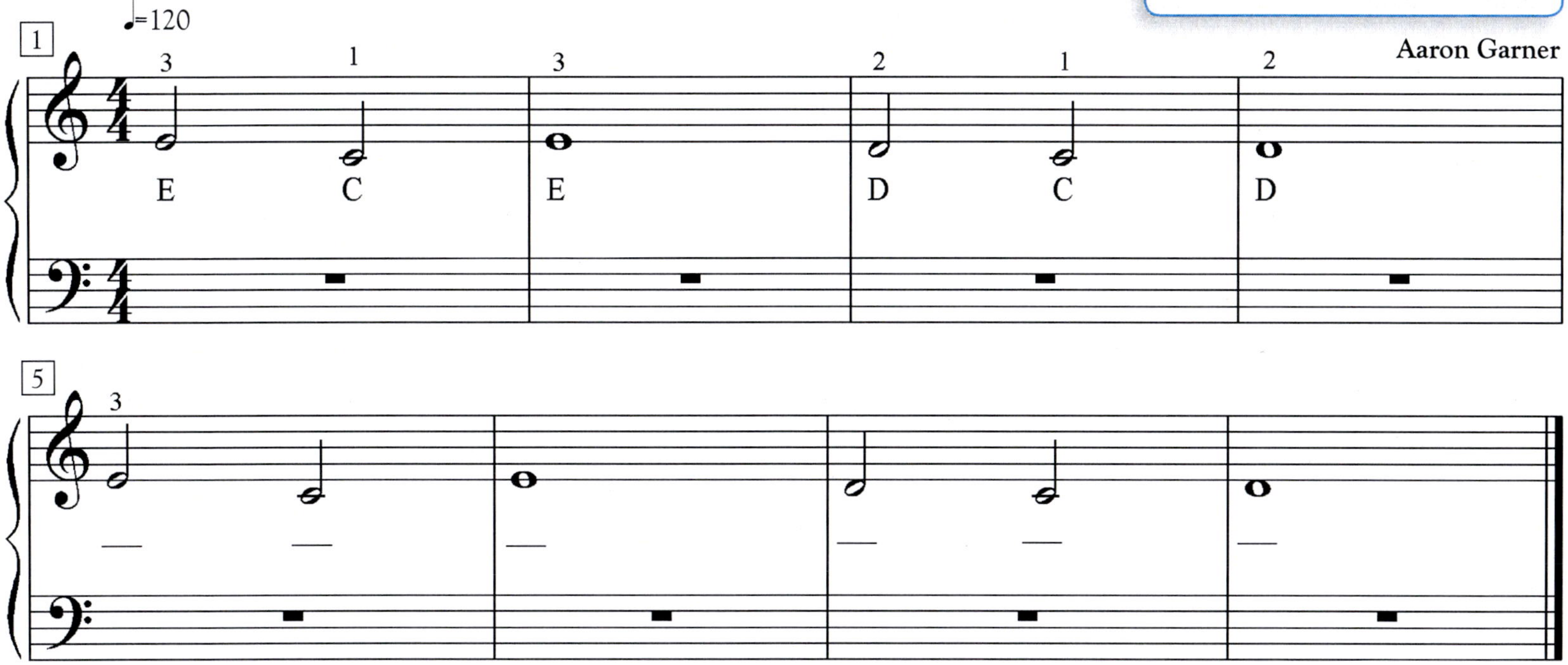

*Student plays 8va

Optional Version on Repeat

PIANO MARVEL 33

Agent ABC

Write note names (2nd line)

Aaron Garner

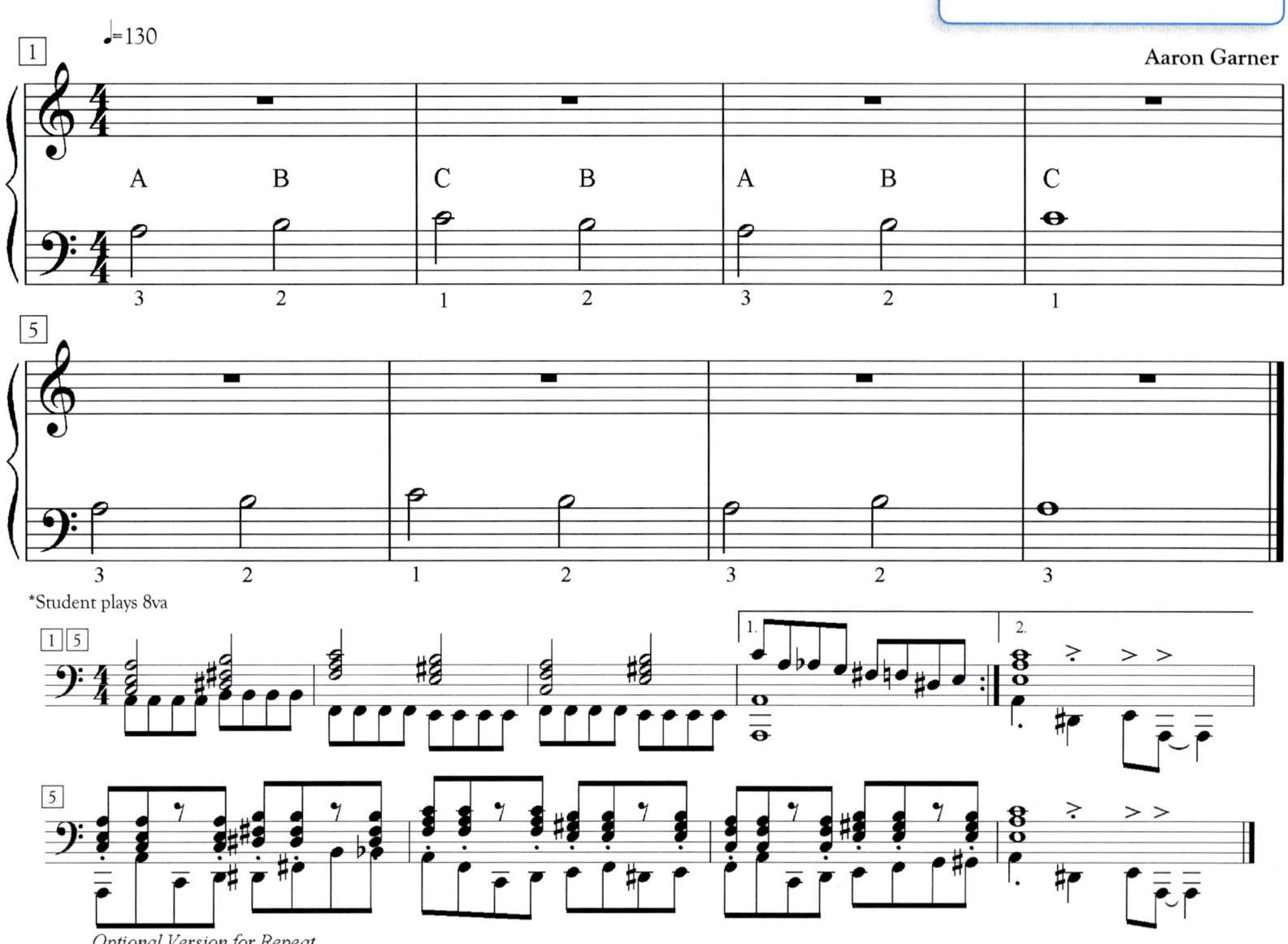

*Student plays 8va

Optional Version for Repeat

34 PIANO MARVEL

© 2011 All Rights Reserved

1B Review

1. Fill in the blanks.

𝄇 = _____ Sign

6/8 _____ counts per measure
     the _____ note gets the count

2. Write the names of the red notes on the lines provided.

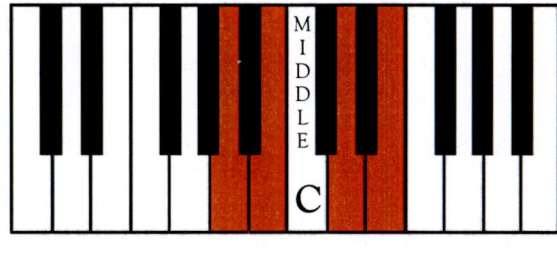

___ ___   ___ ___

3. Write the names of the red notes on the lines provided.

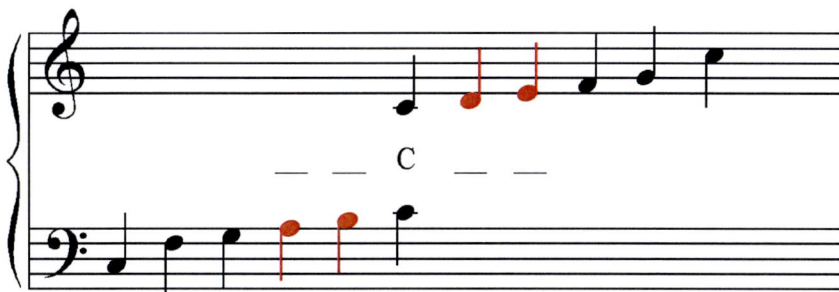

___ ___ C ___ ___

4. Visit pianomarvel.com and take the Standard Assessment of Sight Reading, then record your score.

SASR Score

5. Choose and learn a piece from the online Piano Marvel library.

© 2011 All Rights Reserved

Peter Peter

This is to be learned by rote and not note reading. You can find a video on youtube.com by doing a search for "piano marvel peter peter".

Traditional

Part 3

Teacher Accompaniment

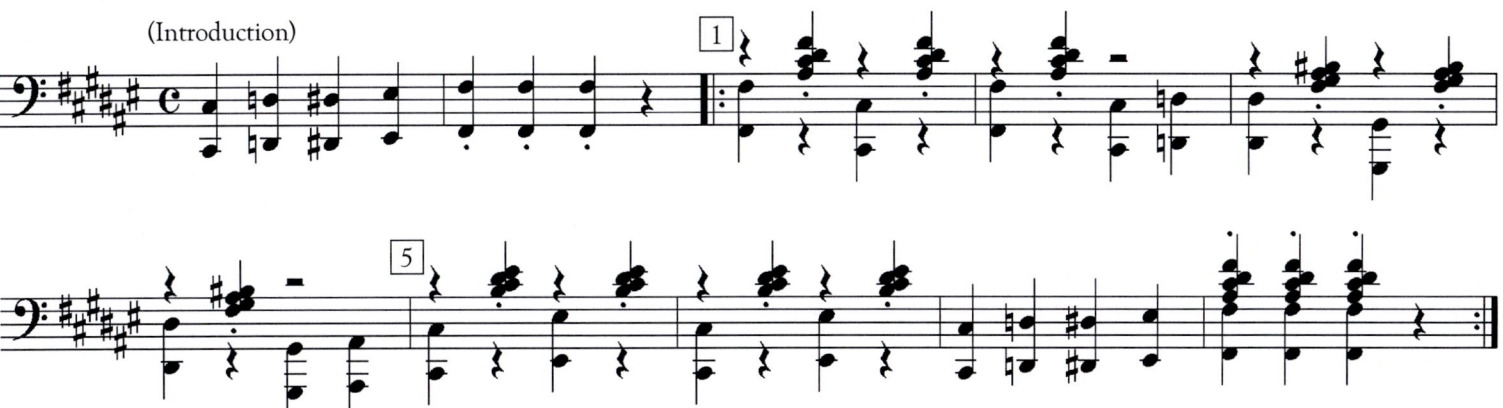

Ice Man

Aaron Garner

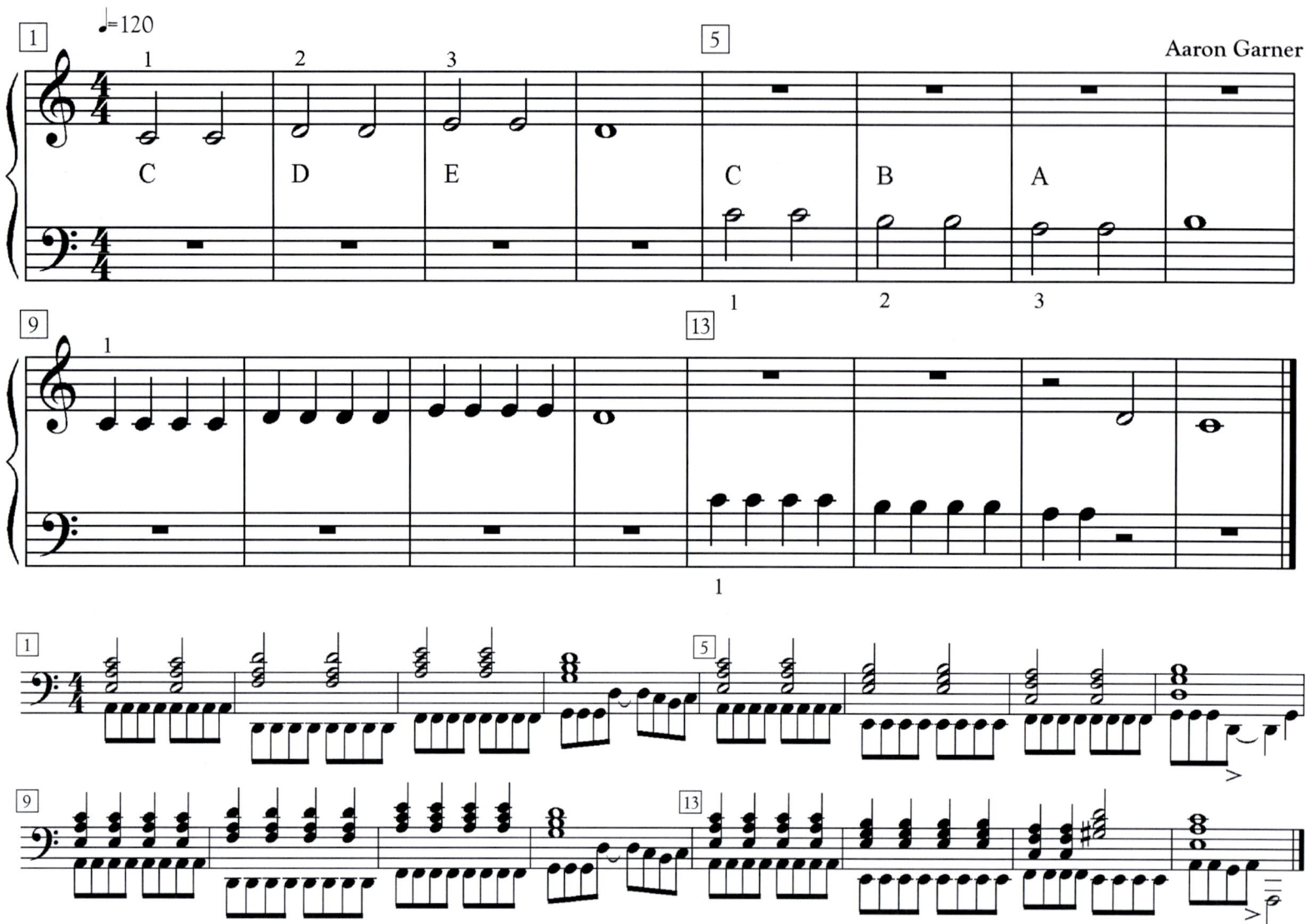

Sands of Time

1. Play and count out loud
2. Write note names (2nd line)

Aaron Garner

Ten Little Indian Rhythm

Clap and count out loud

Aaron Garner

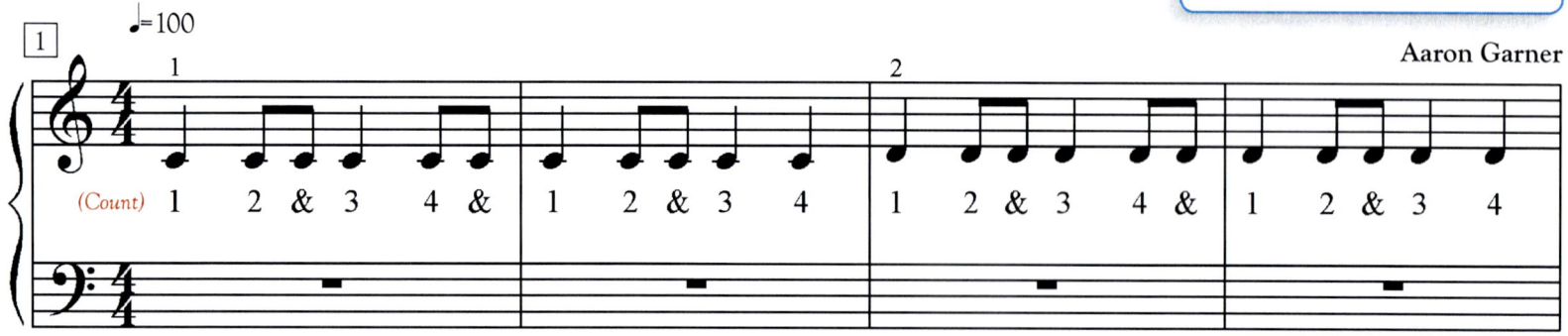

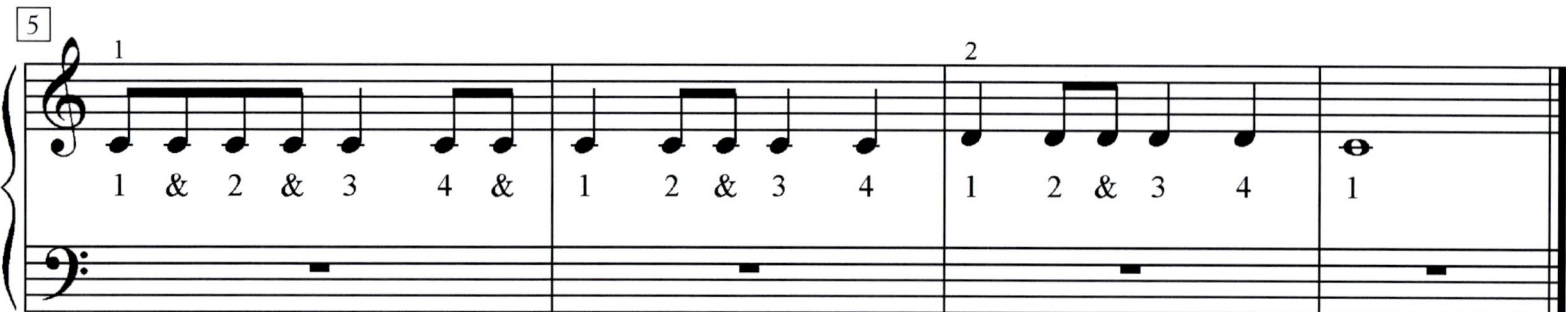

*Student plays 8va

Get Off the Tracks

Indians

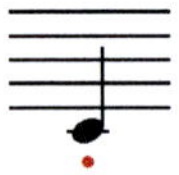

Introduction to Staccatos, Slurs and Legato

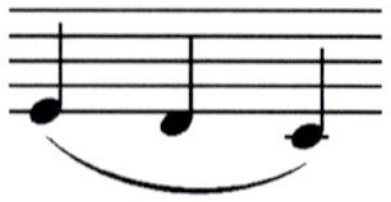

Staccato = short

Legato = smoothly, connected

Slur = curved line indicating the notes should be played **legato**.

Aaron Garner

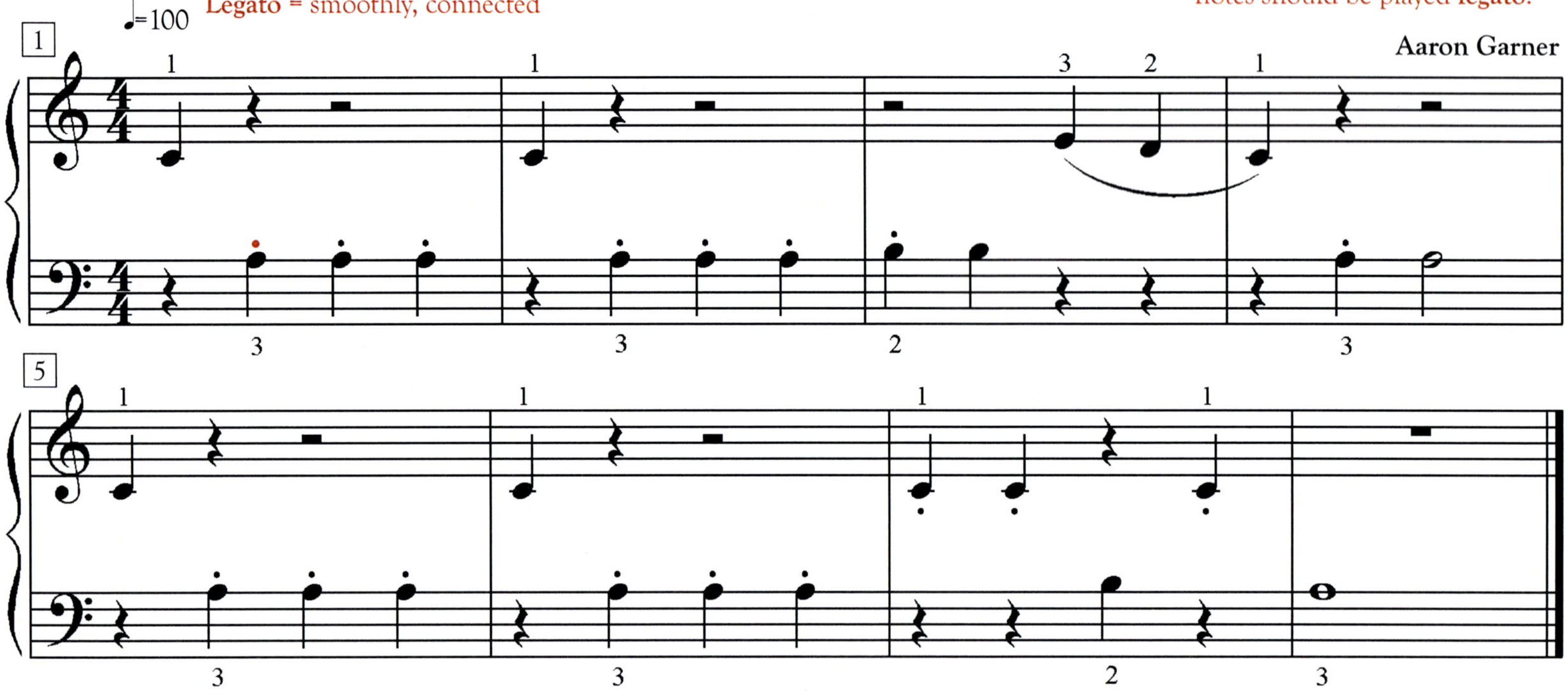

*Student plays 8va

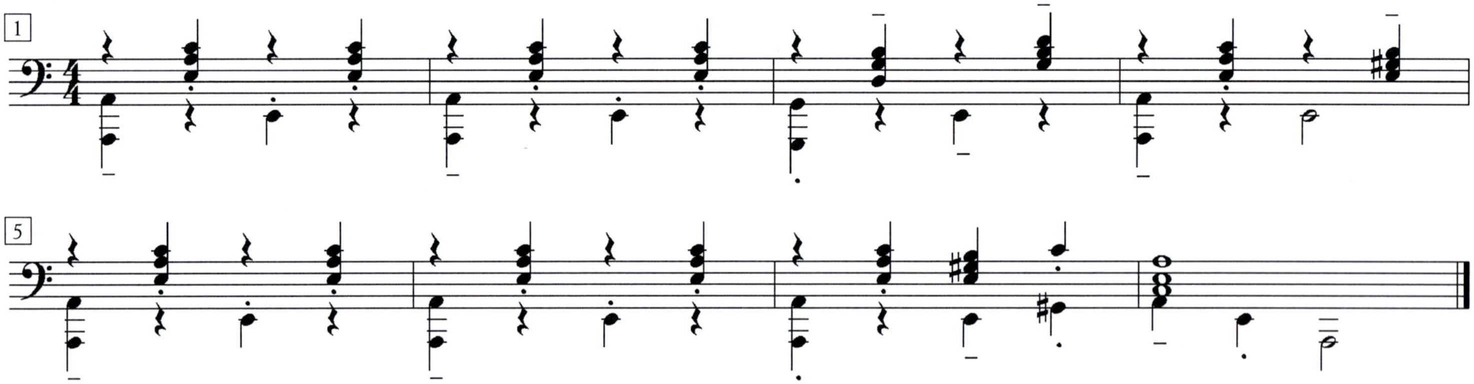

1C Review

1. Write the name of the articulation.

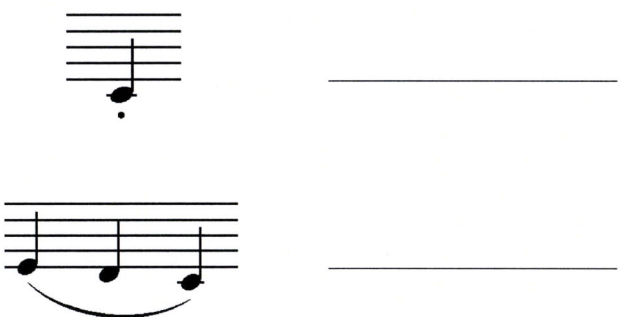

2. Draw a line from the term to its definition.

Staccato   Smooth and connected

Legato   Short and detached

3. Visit pianomarvel.com and take the Standard Assessment of Sight Reading, then record your score.

SASR Score

4. Choose and learn a piece from the online Piano Marvel library.

Quiet Moments (RH)

Introduction to F

Adagio = Slowly

Aaron Garner

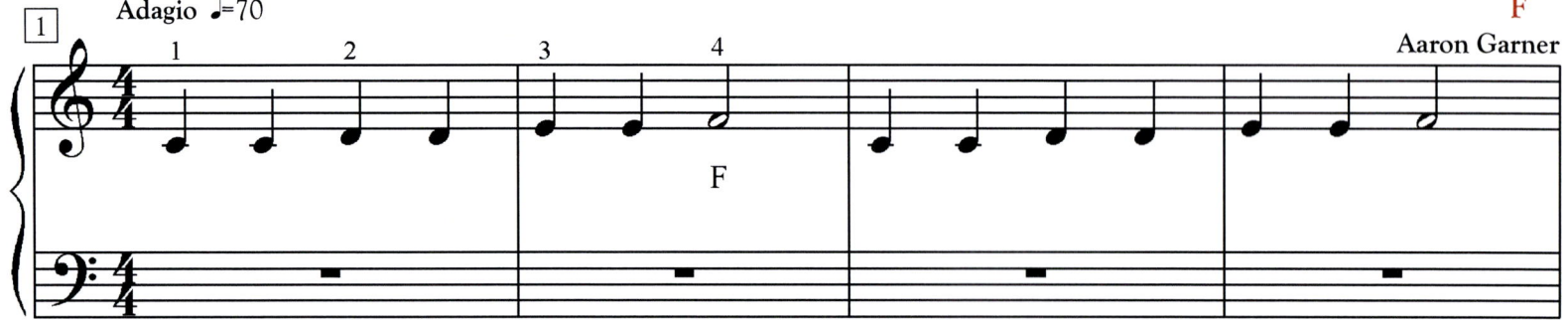
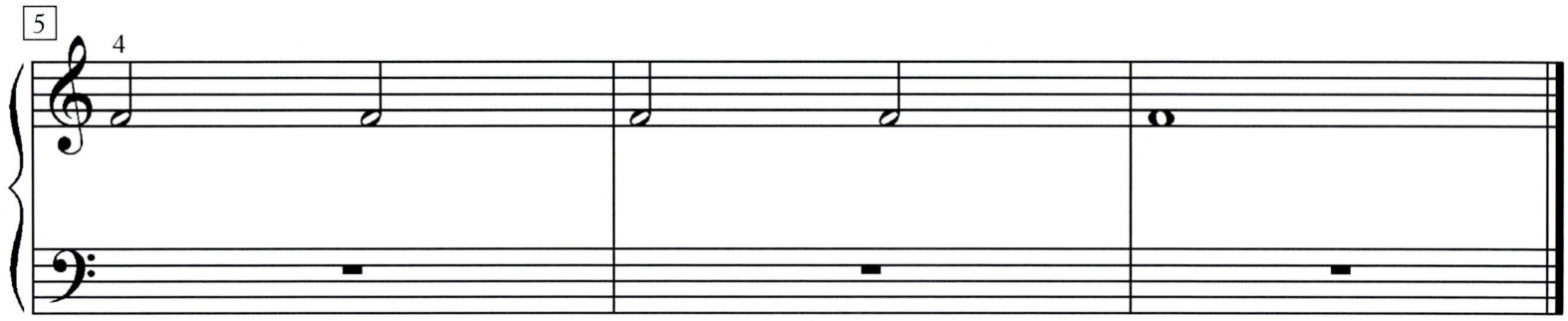

Never Never Land

Allegro = Fast

1. Play and count out loud
2. Write note names

Aaron Garner

*Student plays 8va

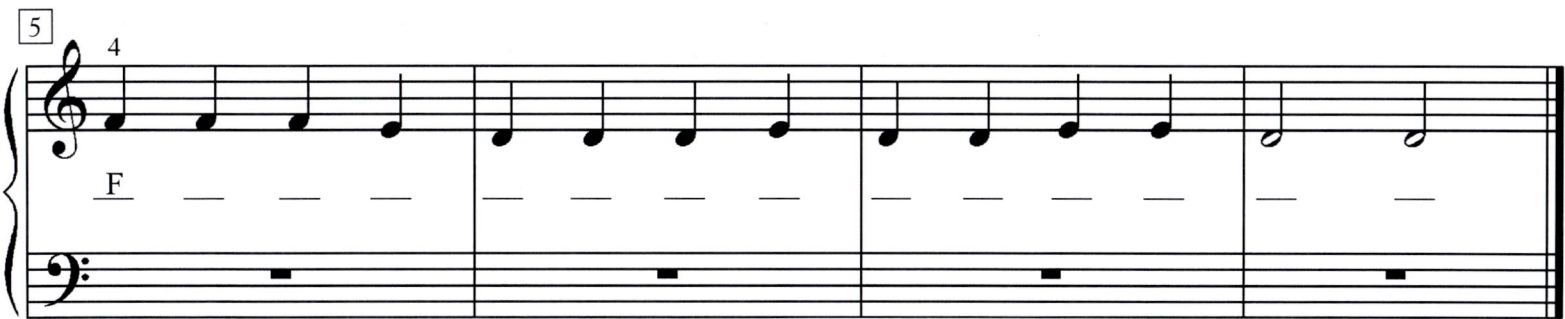

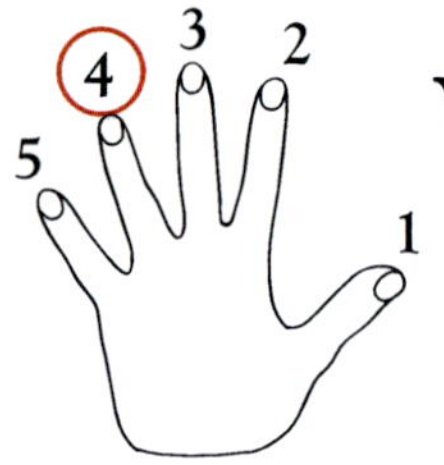

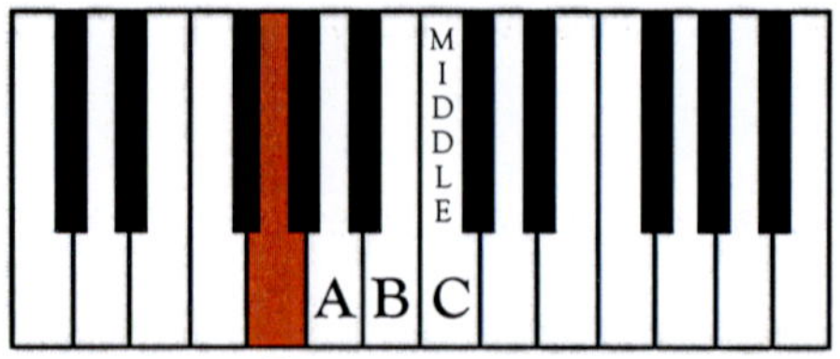

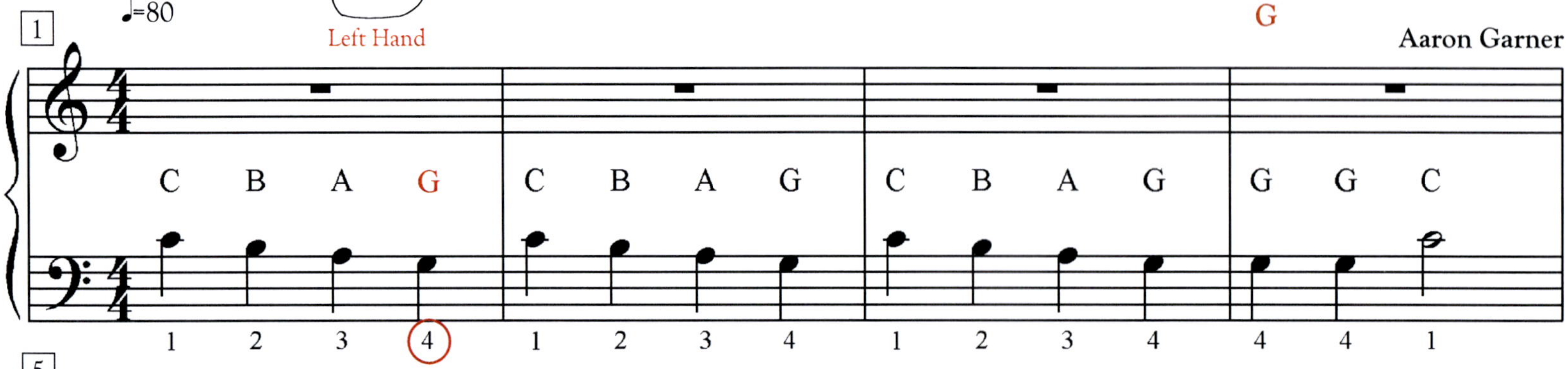

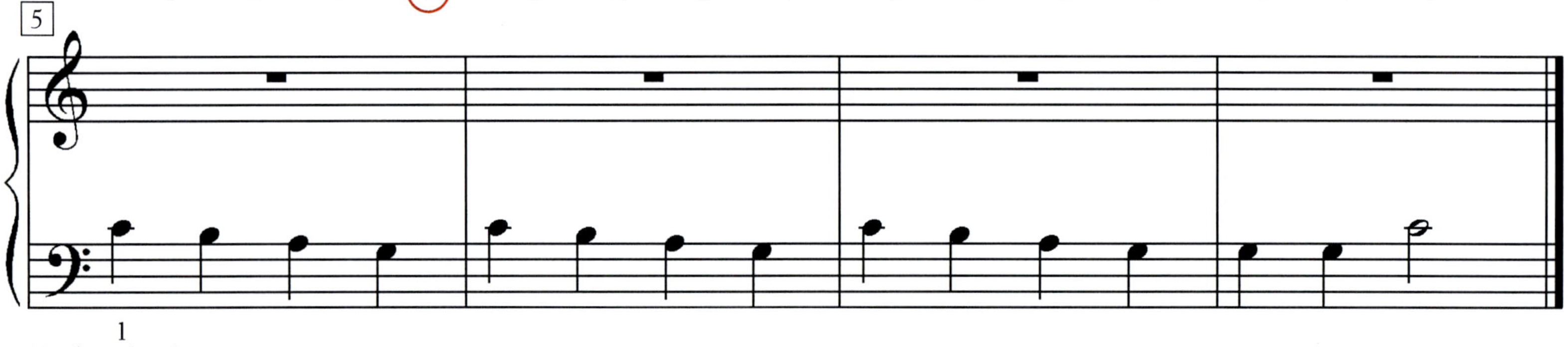

Texas

Mother May I?
Introduction to *f* (forte)

Aaron Garner

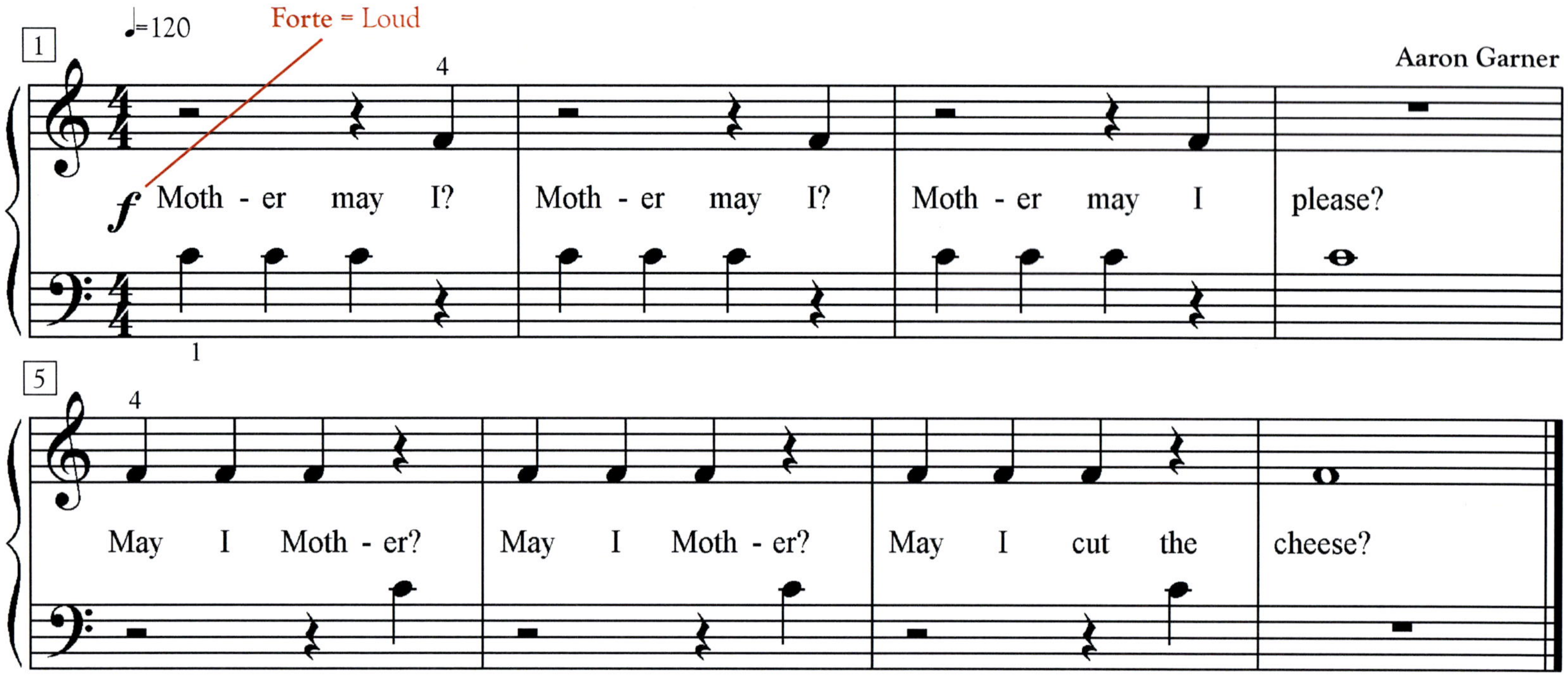

*Student plays 8va

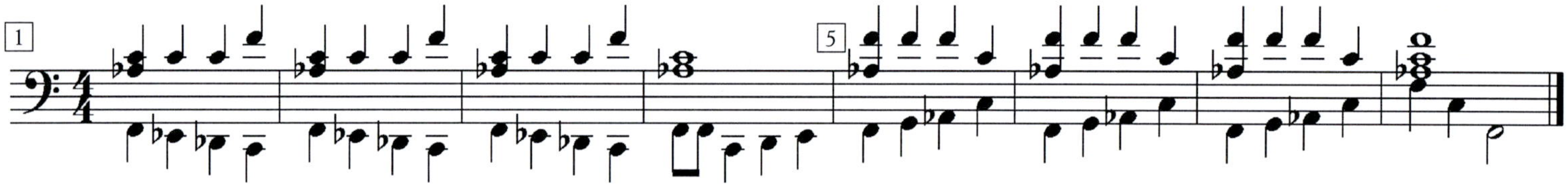

Try replacing the left hand bass line with this optional pattern.

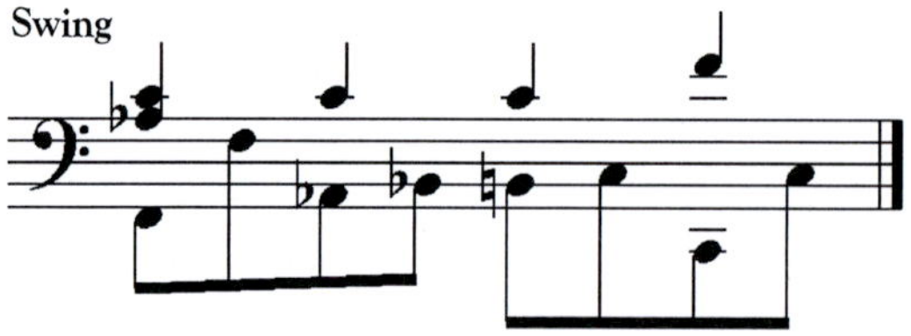

Daytime

Introduction to *p* (piano)

1. Play and count out loud
2. Play and name the notes

Aaron Garner

*Student plays 8va

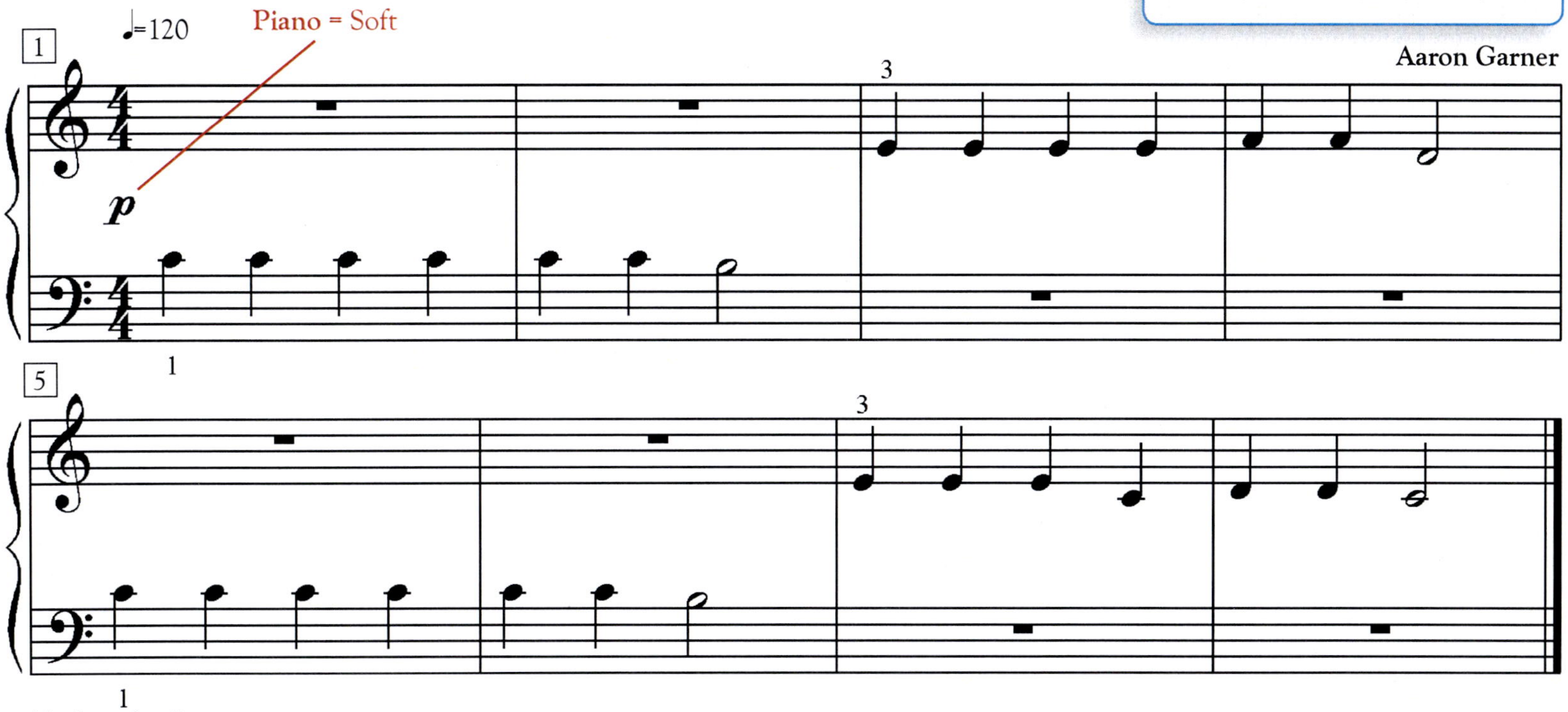

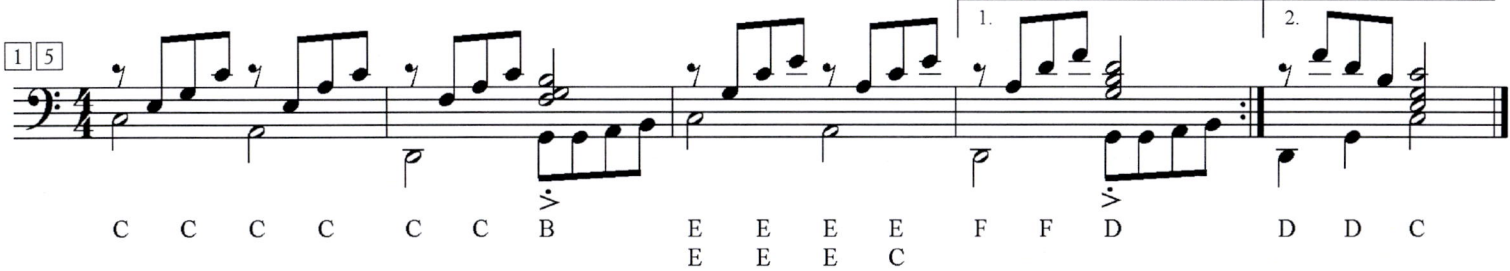

Yankee Doodle

The Dotted Half Note
Introduction to the Dotted Half Note

𝅗𝅥. = 3 beats

Clap and count out loud

Aaron Garner

*Student plays 8va

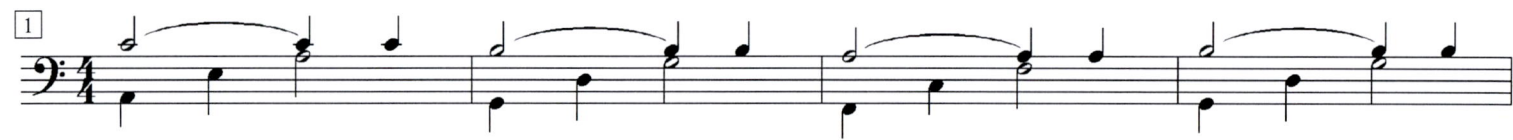

♩. = 1½ beats

♪ = ½ beat

The Dotted Quarter Note

Introduction to the Dotted Quarter & Eighth Note

Aaron Garner

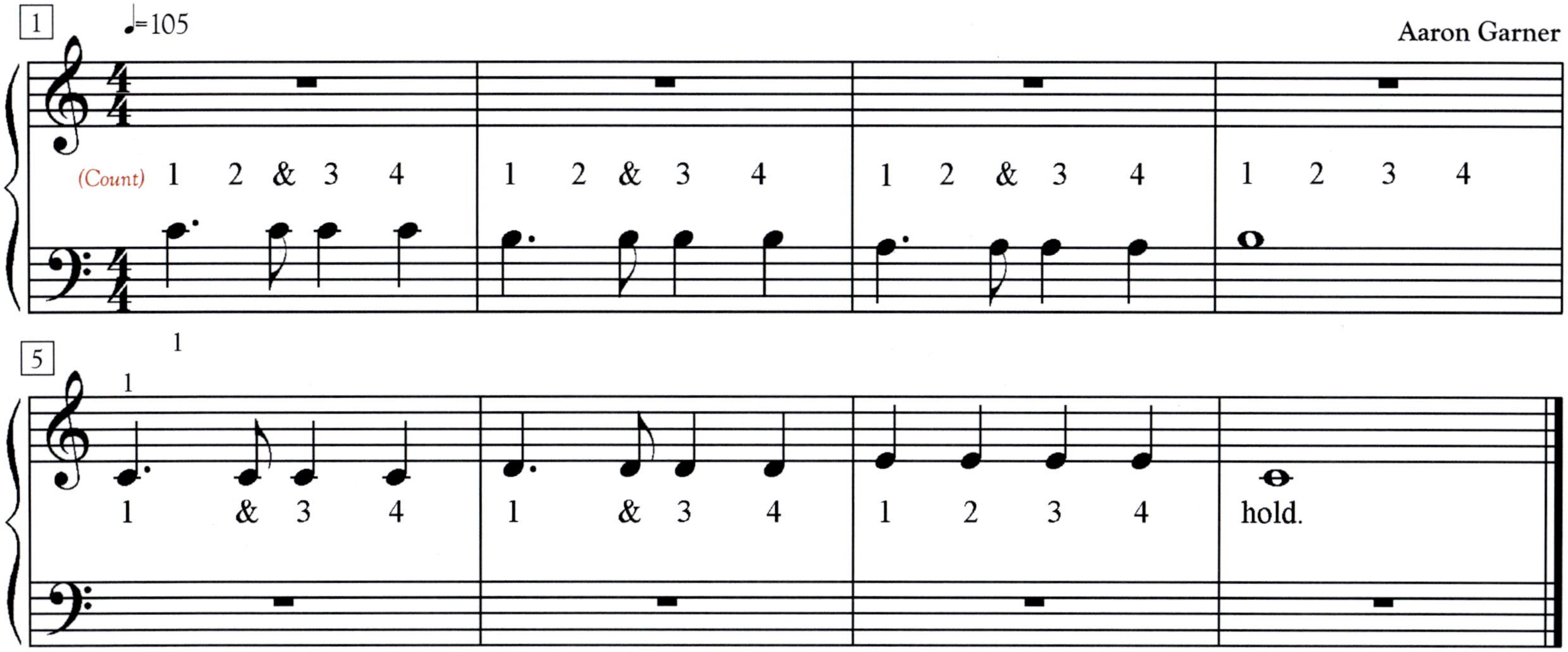

*Student plays 8va

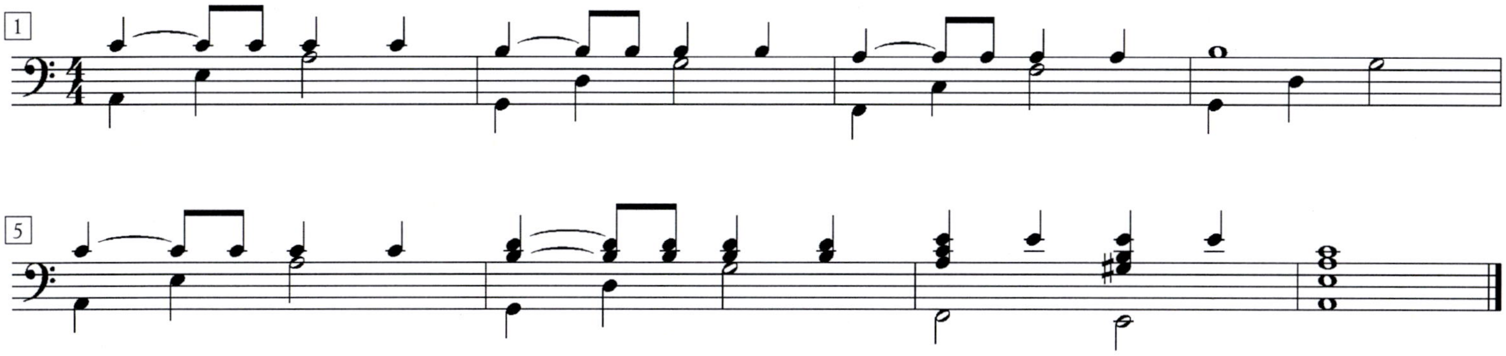

Lion Soup

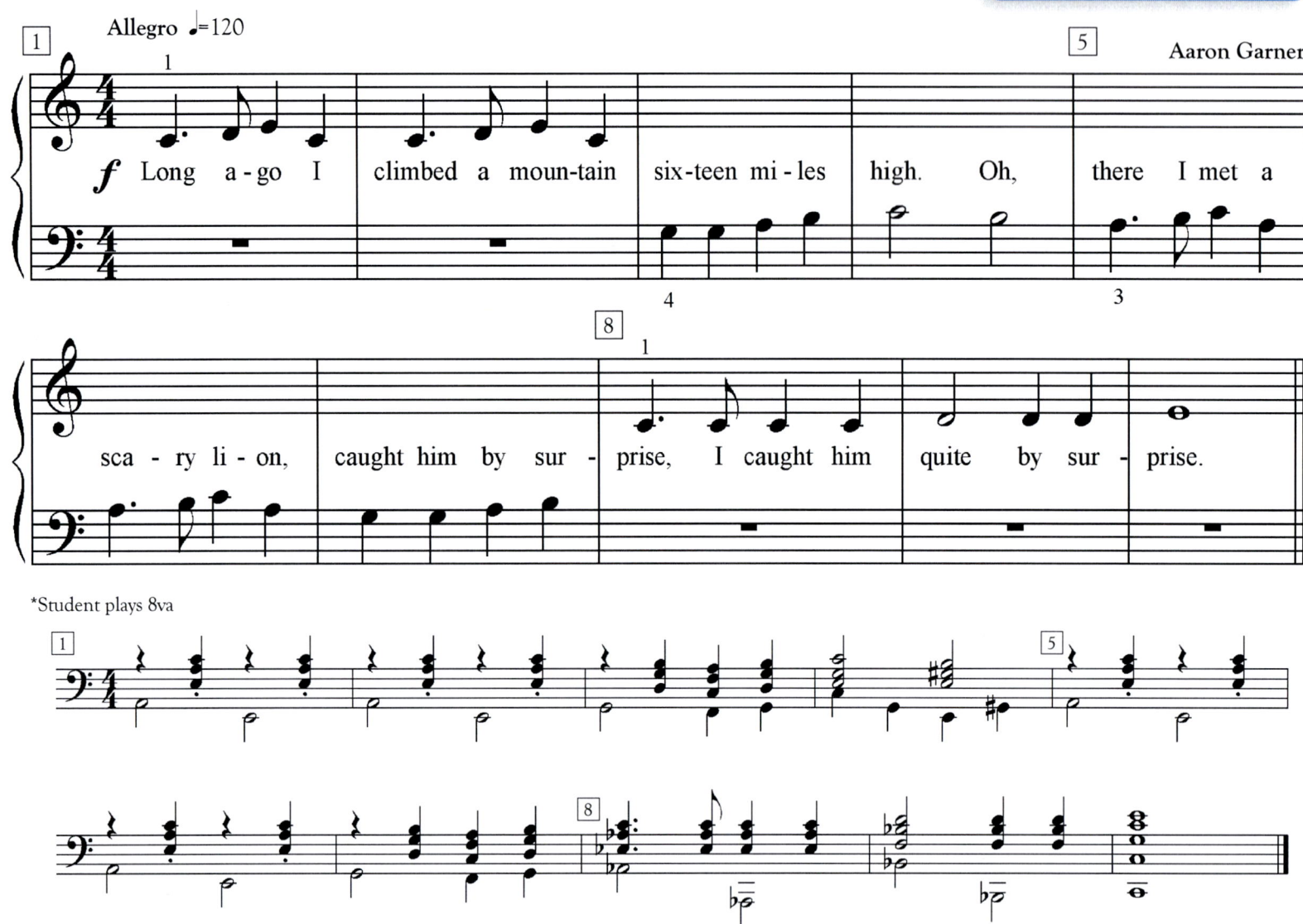

Tied Notes

Solemn Reflections
Introduction to Tied Notes

Clap and count out loud

1D

Aaron Garner

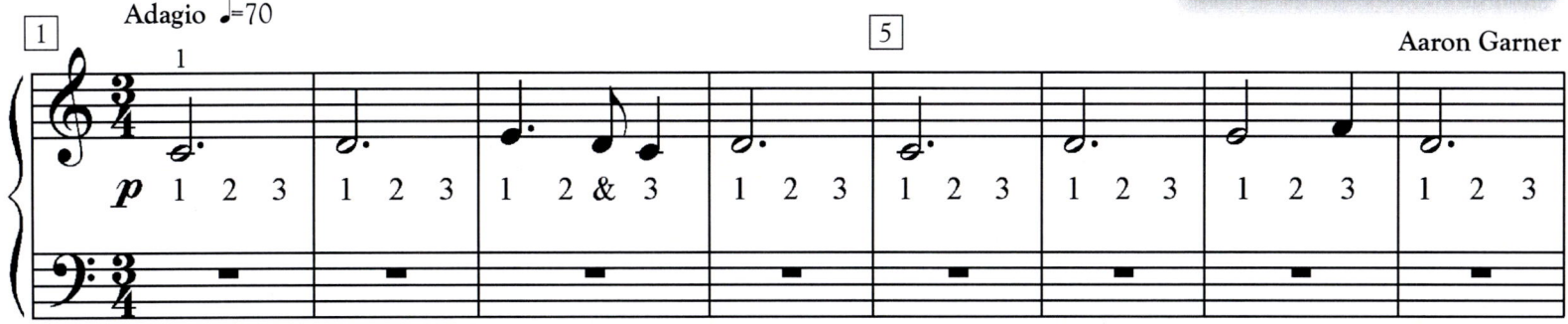

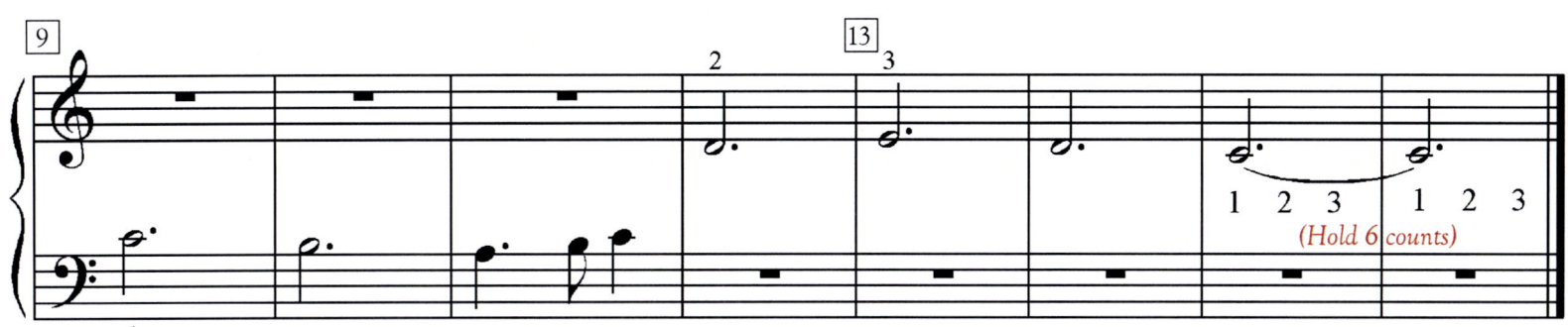

*Student plays 8va

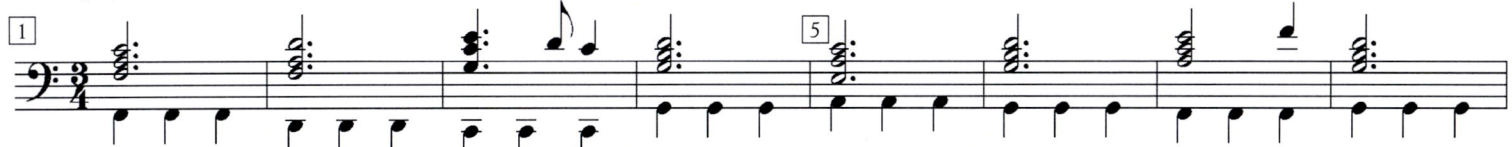

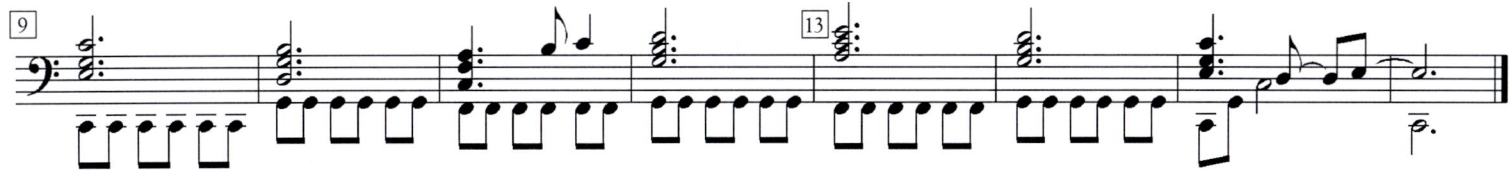

PIANO MARVEL **55**

1D Review

1. Point to each measure in order. How many measures are there? ____

2. Write the names of the red notes on the lines provided.

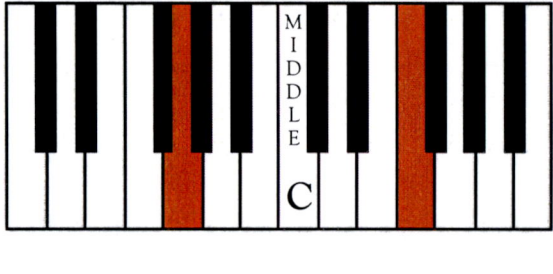

3. Write the names of the red notes on the lines provided.

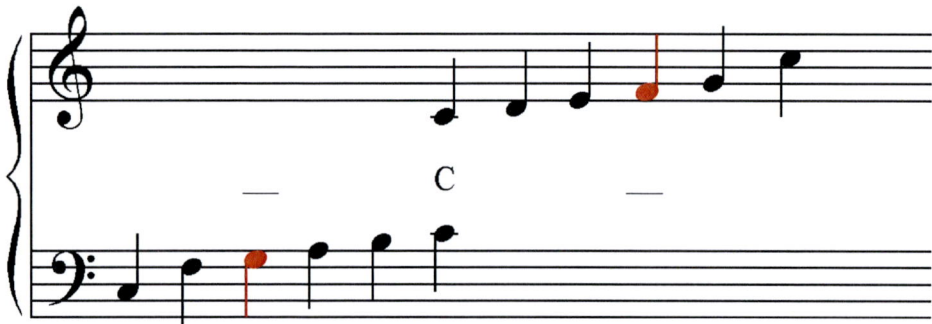

4. Match the symbol or term with the correct definition.

1. ♪ _____Tied Notes

2. *p* _____Slow

3. 𝅗𝅥. _____Piano (soft)

4. Adagio _____Dotted Quarter Note (1 ½ beats)

5. *f* _____Fast

6. Allegro _____Eighth Note (½ beat)

7. [two dotted half notes tied] _____Forte (loud)

8. 𝅗𝅥. _____Dotted Half Note (3 beats)

5. Visit pianomarvel.com and take the Standard Assessment of Sight Reading, then record your score.

SASR Score

6. Choose and learn a piece from the online Piano Marvel library.

1E

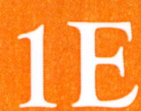

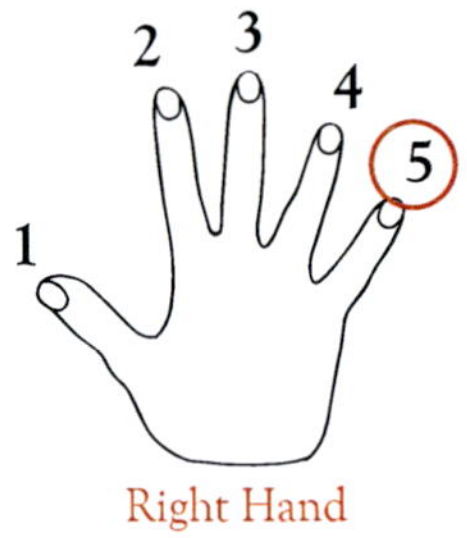

Jupiter

Introduction to G

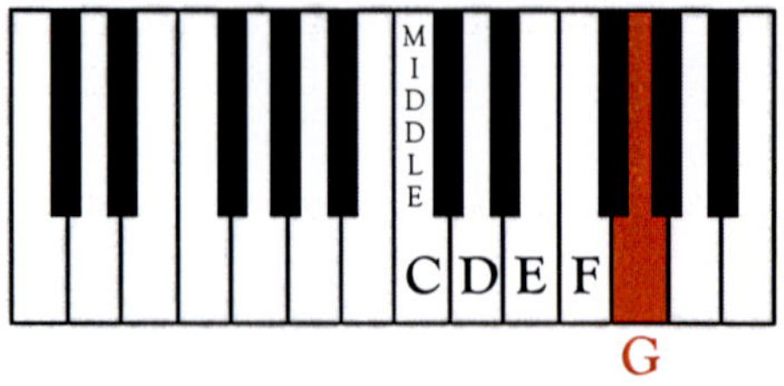

Aaron Garner

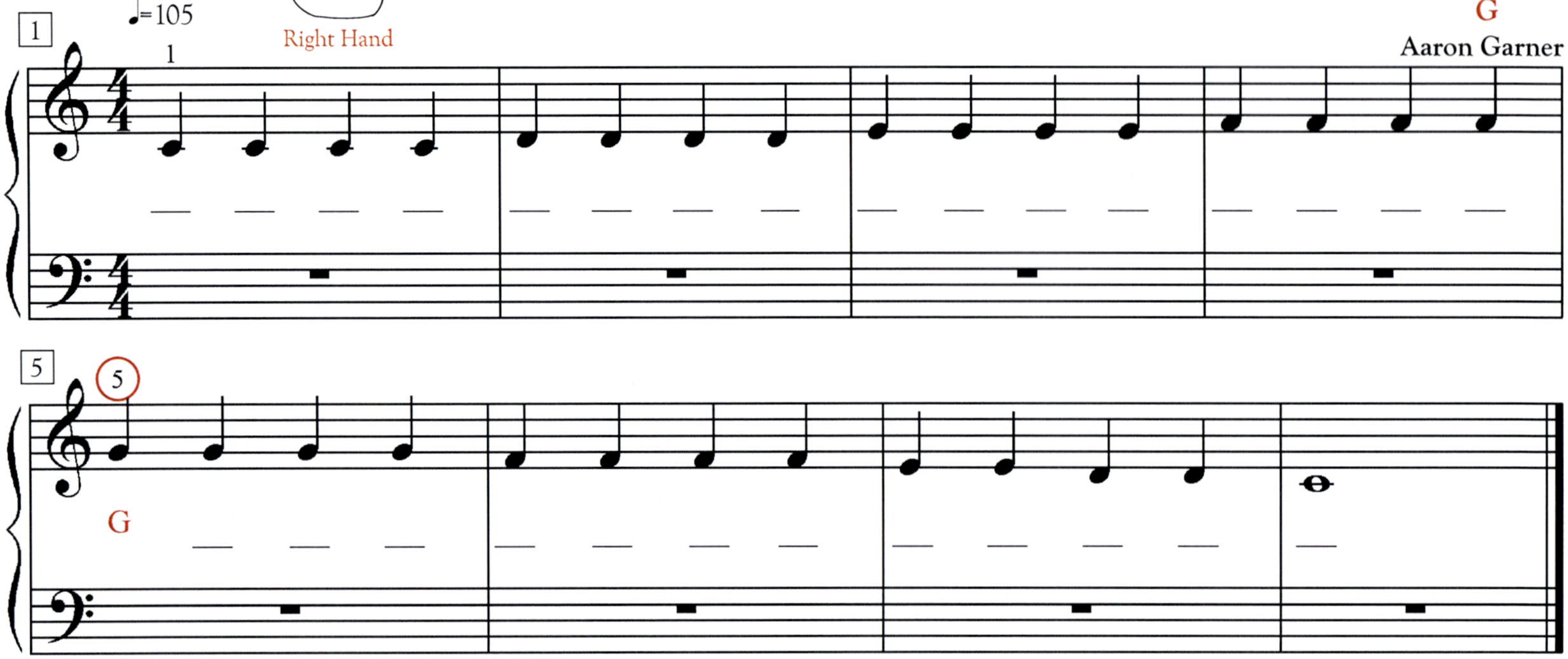

*Student plays 15ma

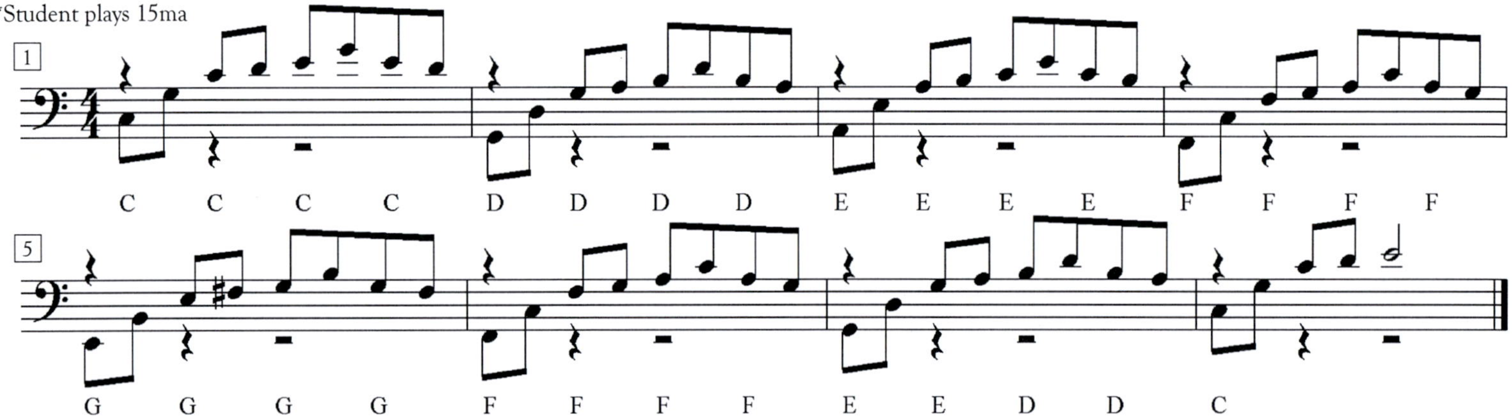

Saturn

For both pages...
1. Write the note names
2. Play and sing the note names

Aaron Garner

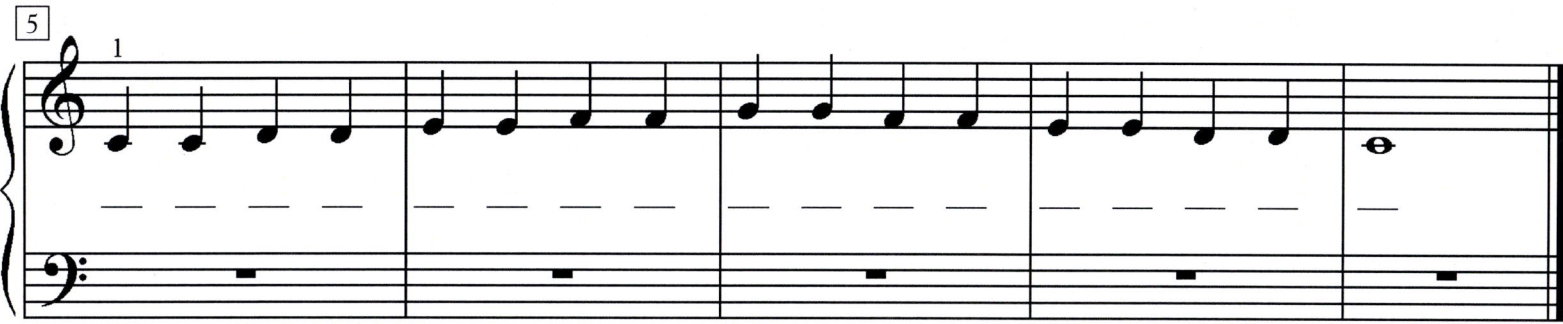

*Student plays 15ma

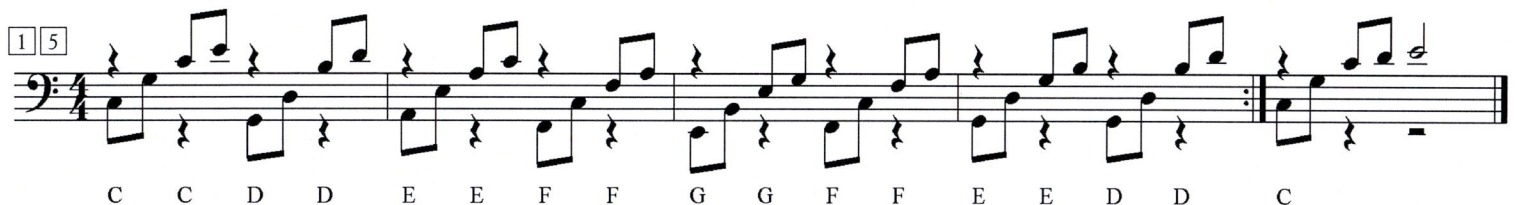

C C D D E E F F G G F F E E D D C

Uranus

For both pages...
1. Write the note names
2. Play and sing the note names

Aaron Garner

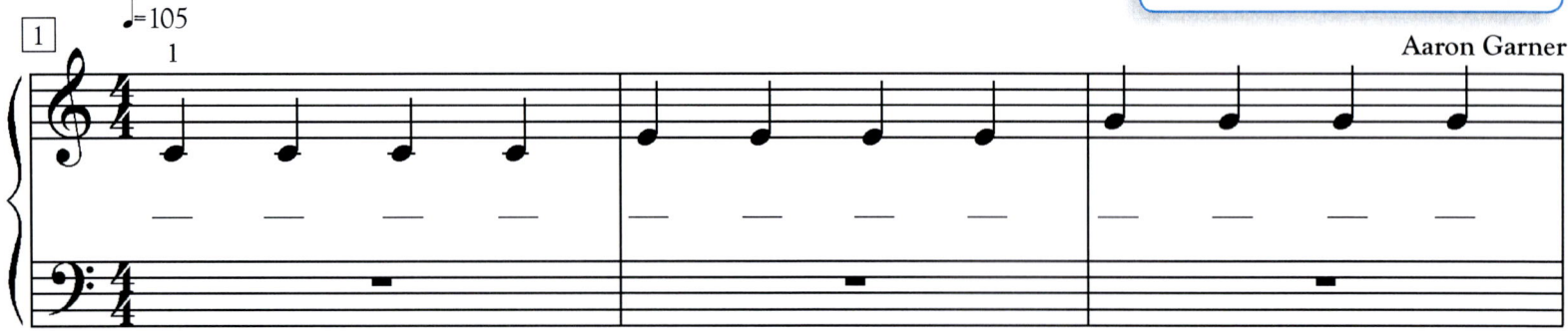

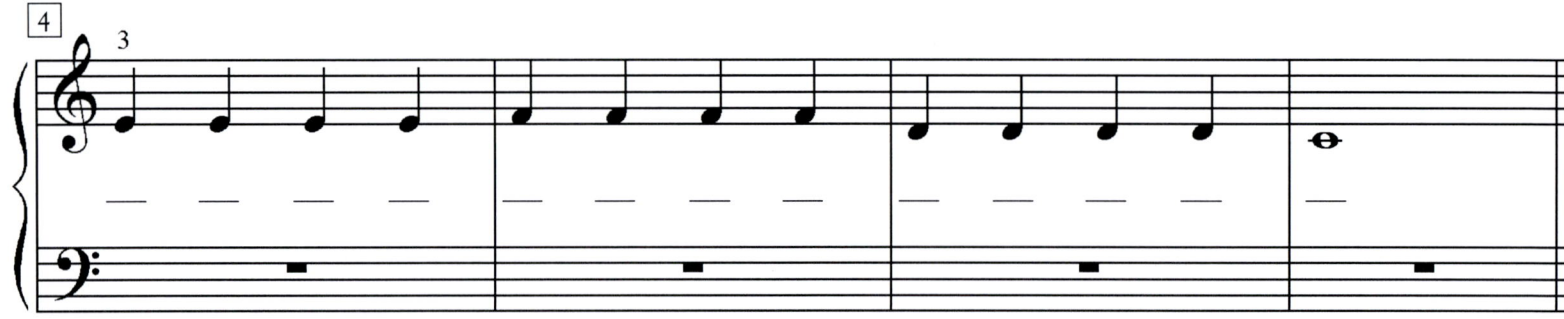

*Student plays 15ma

Neptune

Aaron Garner

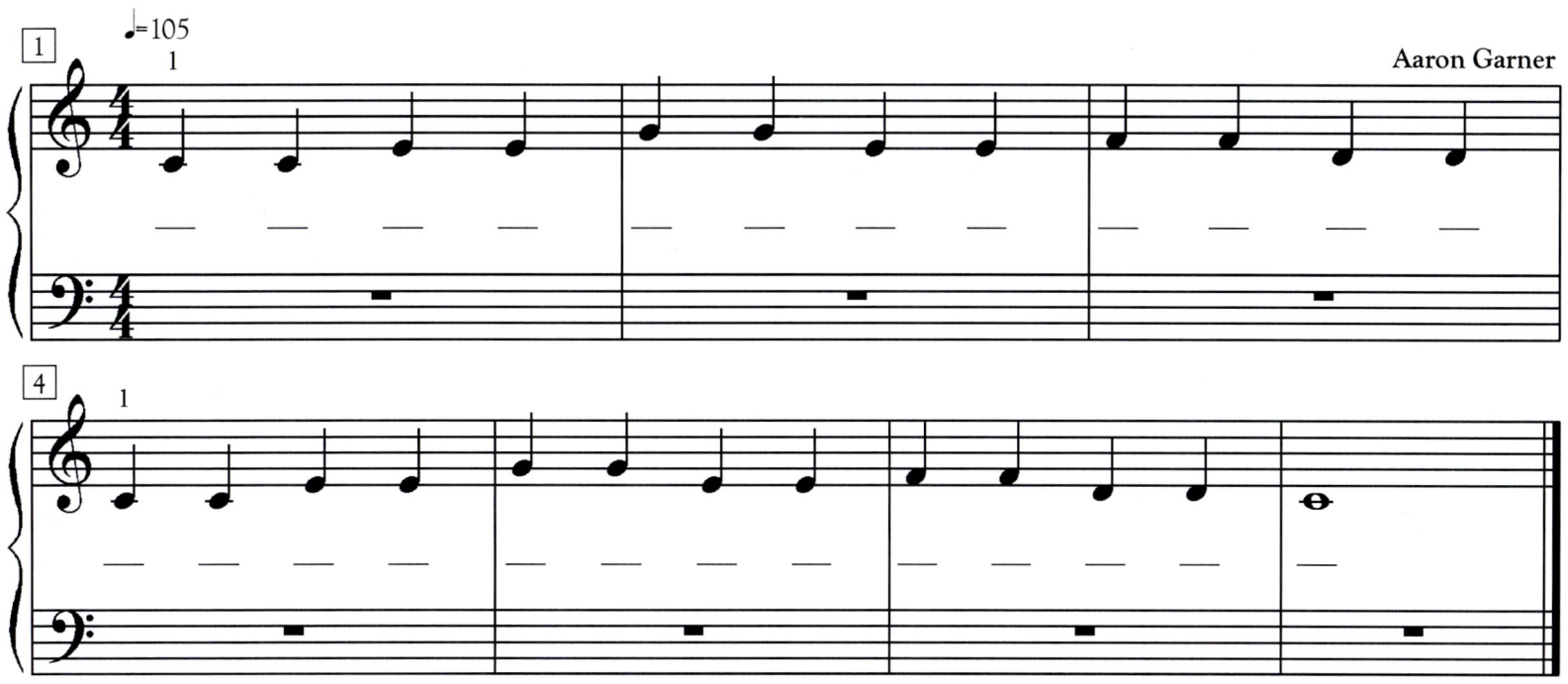

*Student plays 15ma

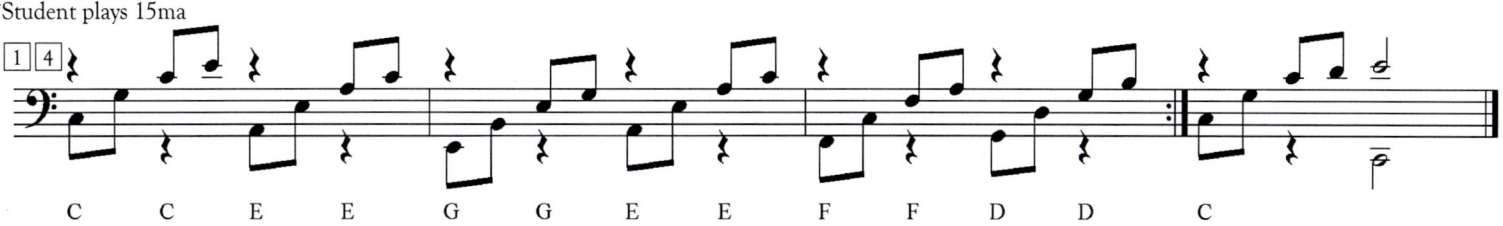

Earth

> 1. Write the note names
> 2. Play and sing the note names

Aaron Garner

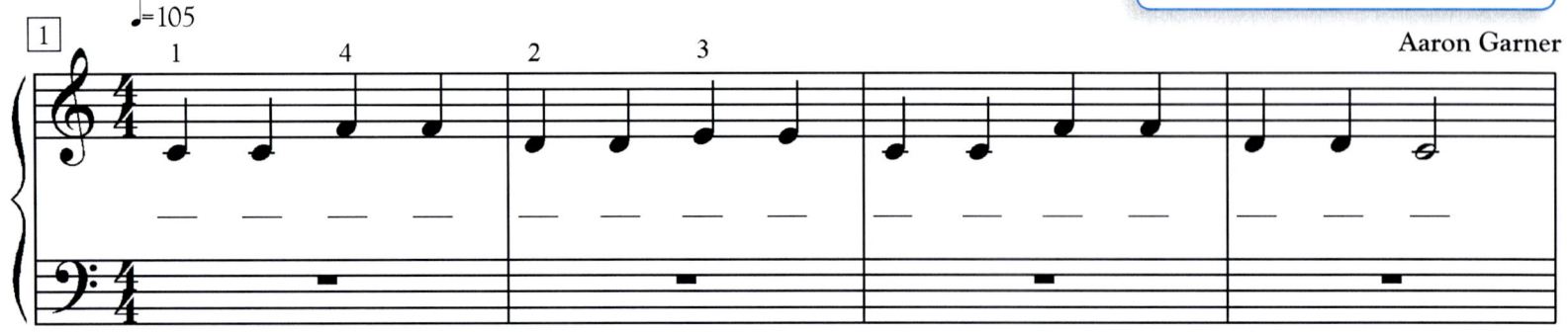
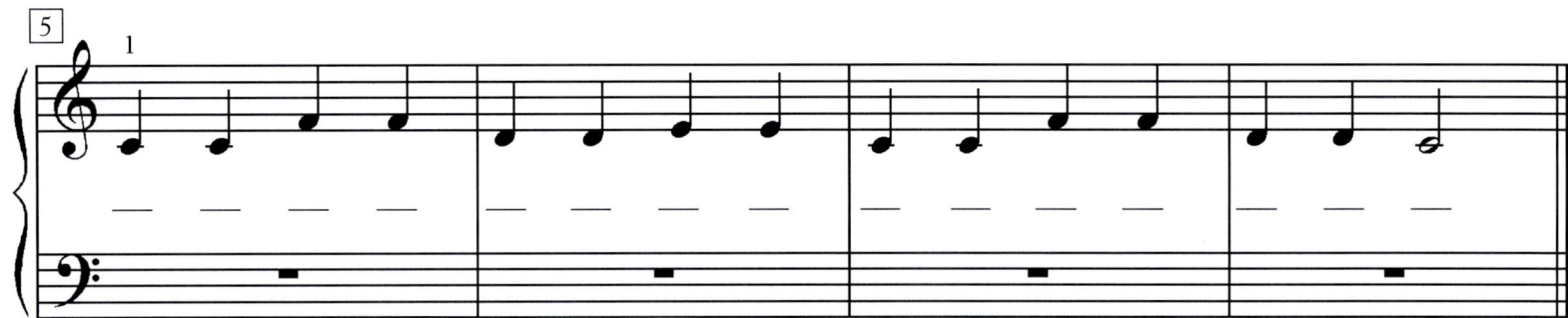

*Student plays 15ma

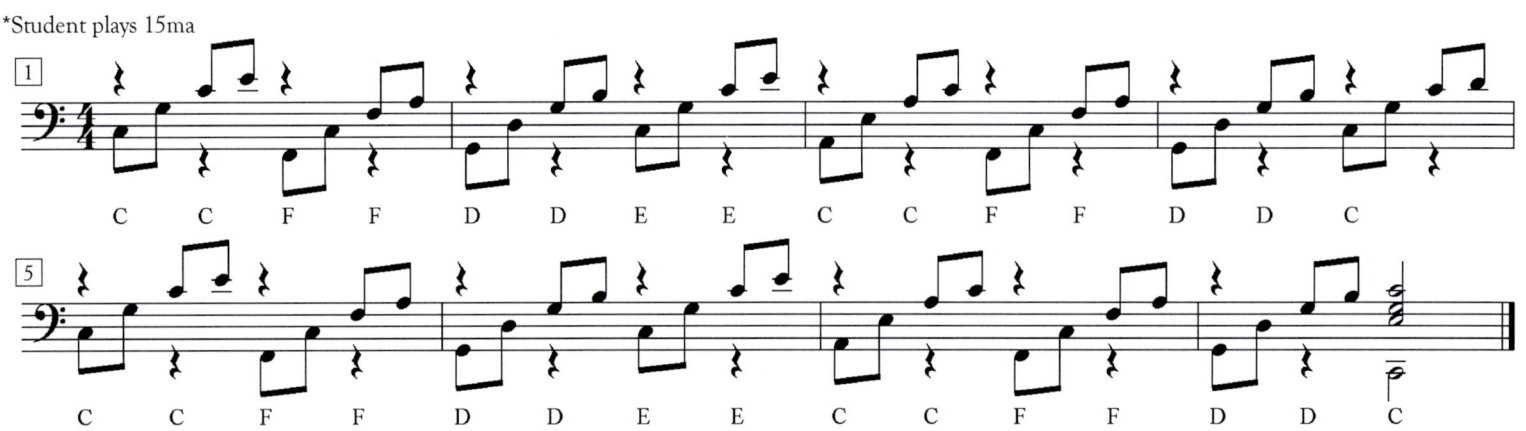

Pirates

Aaron Garner

*Student plays 8va

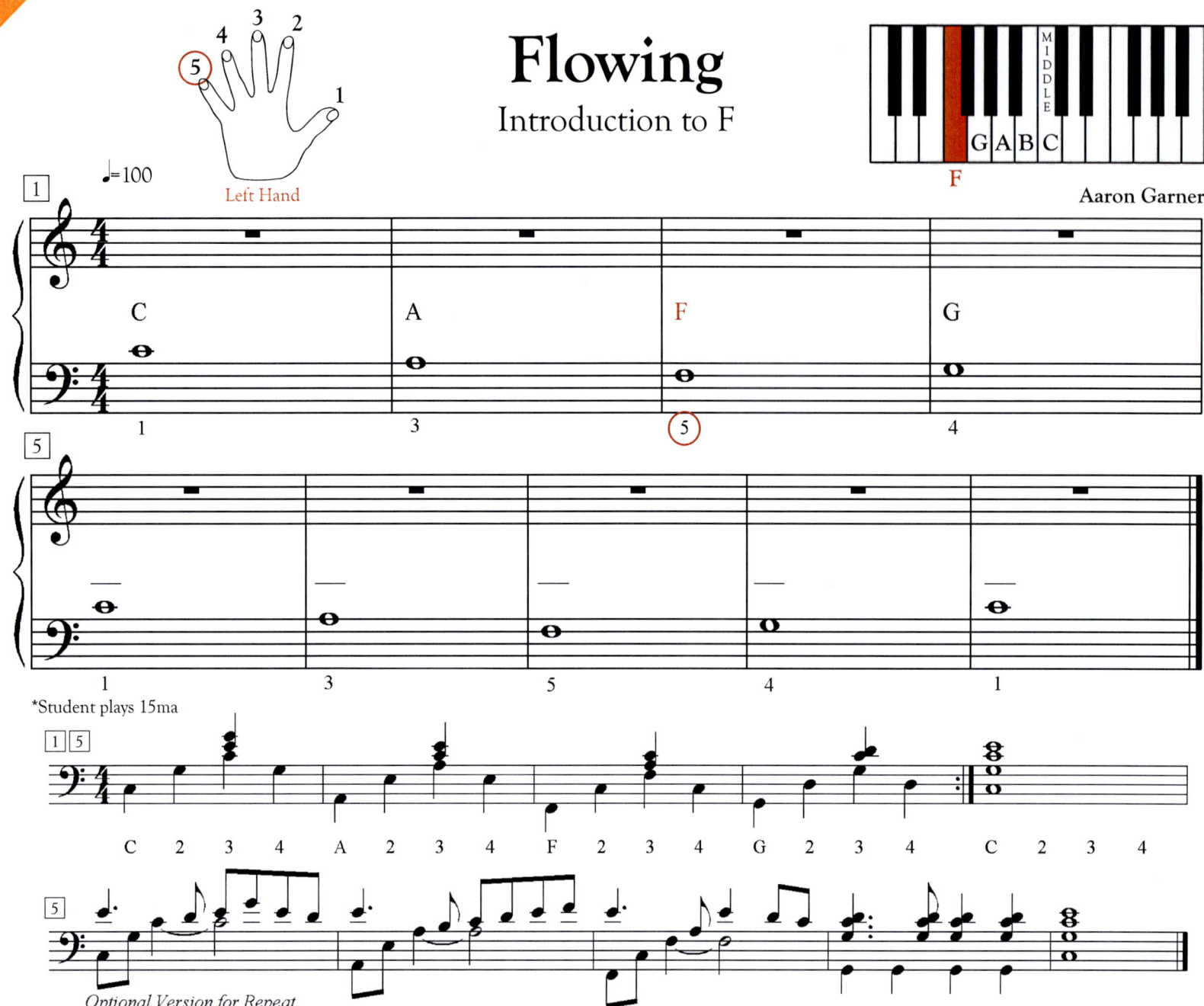

Waters

For both pages...
1. Write the note names
2. Play and sing the note names

Aaron Garner

*Student plays 8va

Optional Version for Repeat

Trickle

Aaron Garner

For both pages...
1. Write the note names
2. Play and sing the note names

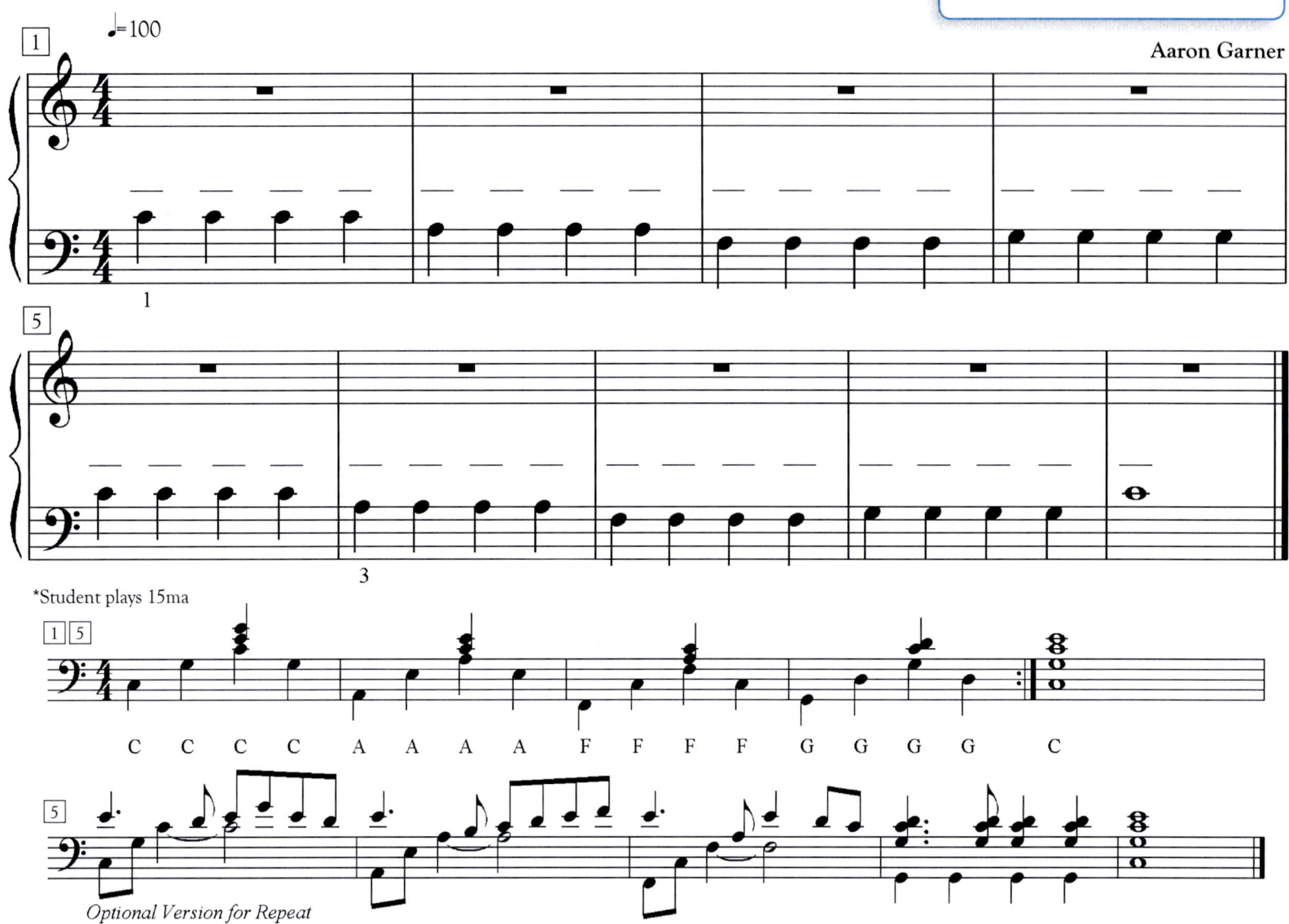

Endlessly

Aaron Garner

*Student plays 15ma

Optional Version for Repeat

Away

1. Write the note names
2. Play and sing the note names

Aaron Garner

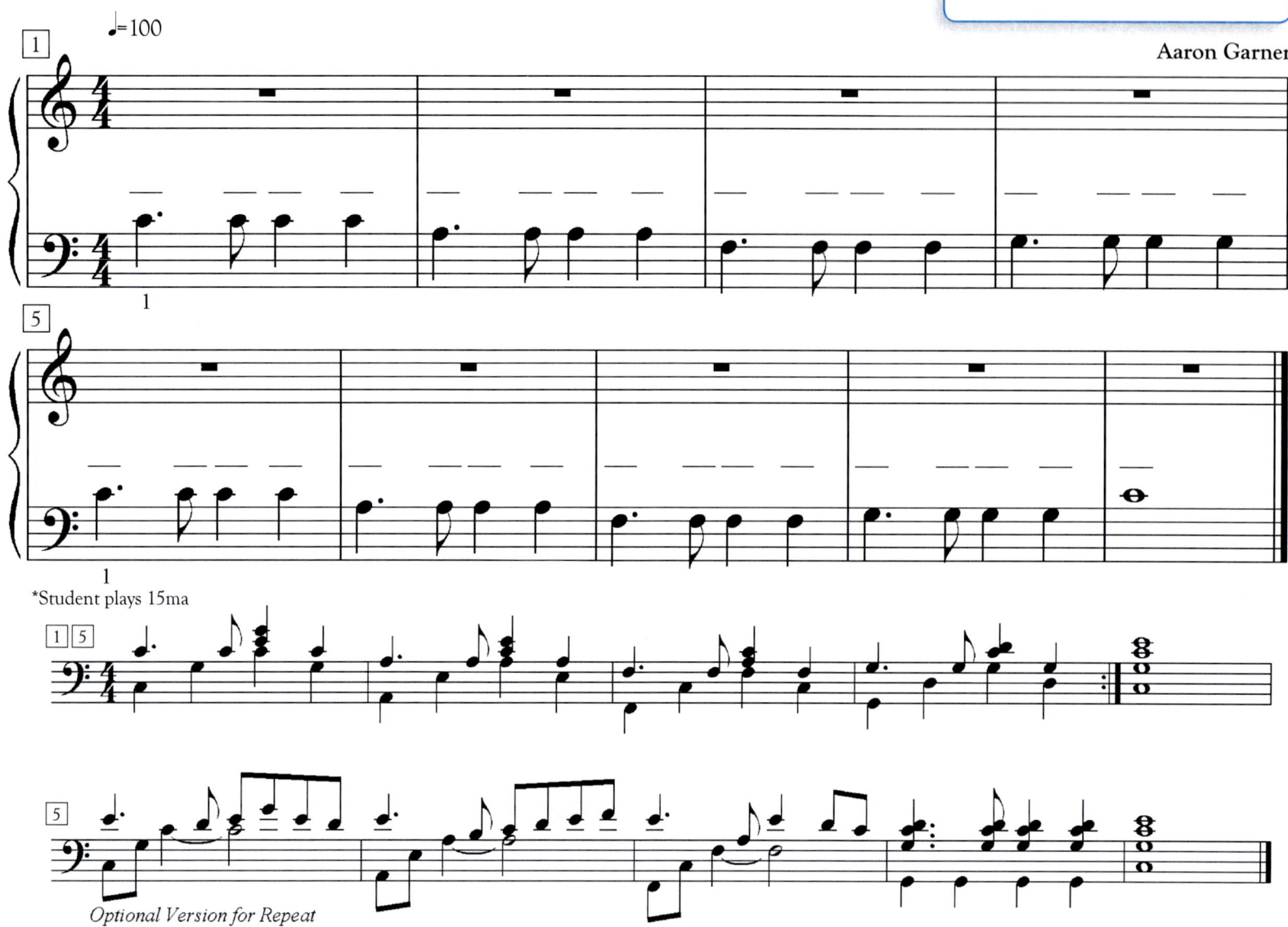

*Student plays 15ma

Optional Version for Repeat

Camptown Races

Old MacDonald
Teacher Accompaniment

♩=110

*Student plays 8va

Straight

Old Mac-Don-ald had a farm, E - I - E - I - O
On that farm he had a pig, E - I - E - I - O

Oink oink here, oink oink there, here an oink, there an oink ev-'ry-where an oink oink

Old Mac-Don-ald had a farm, E - I - E - I - O.

Swing

Old__ Mac - Don - ald__ had__ a__ farm, E - I - E - I - O__
On__ that__ farm__ he__ had__ a__ pig, E - I - E - I - O__

Oink oink here, oink oink there, here an oink, there an oink ev-'ry-where an oink oink

To Coda

D.C. al Coda

Old MacDonald

1E Review

1. Write the names of the red notes on the lines provided.

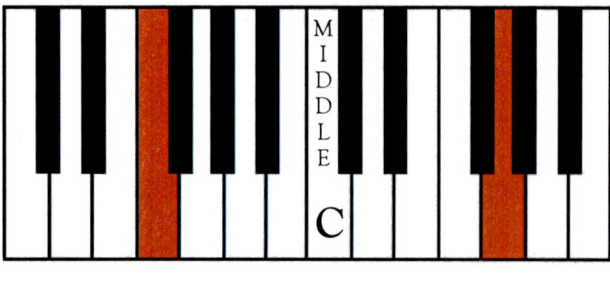

2. Write the names of the red notes on the lines provided.

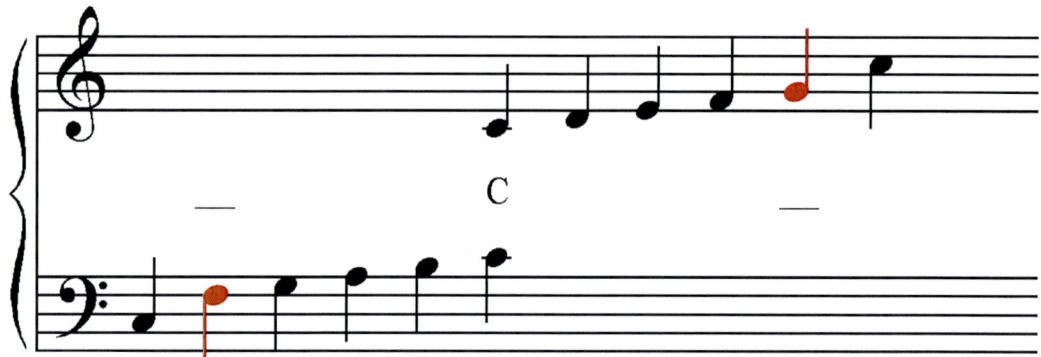

Note Value Test

3. Match the symbol with the correct definition.

1. 𝐨   _____ Double Eighth Note

2. ▬   _____ Quarter Rest

3. 𝅗𝅥   _____ Single Eighth Note

4. ▬   _____ Half Rest

5. ♩   _____ Half Note

6. 𝄽   _____ Whole Rest

7. ♫   _____ Quarter Note

8. ♪   _____ Whole Note

4. Visit pianomarvel.com and take the Standard Assessment of Sight Reading, then record your score.

SASR Score

5. Choose and learn a piece from the online Piano Marvel library.

© 2011 All Rights Reserved

Terms & Signs Test

Match the symbol or term with the correct definition.

1. **Adagio**
2. 𝄞
3. ♩ (staccato note)
4. (slurred notes)
5. **Allegro**
6. (1st & 2nd ending example)
7. *p*
8. *f*
9. (repeat sign)
10. (tied notes example)
11. 𝄢

_____ Soft

_____ Fast

_____ Loud

_____ Tied Notes

_____ Slow

_____ Staccato

_____ Treble Clef

_____ Slur

_____ Bass Clef

_____ Repeat Sign

_____ 1st & 2nd Ending

74 PIANO MARVEL

© 2011 All Rights Reserved

Grand Staff Test

Write the term on the correct line.

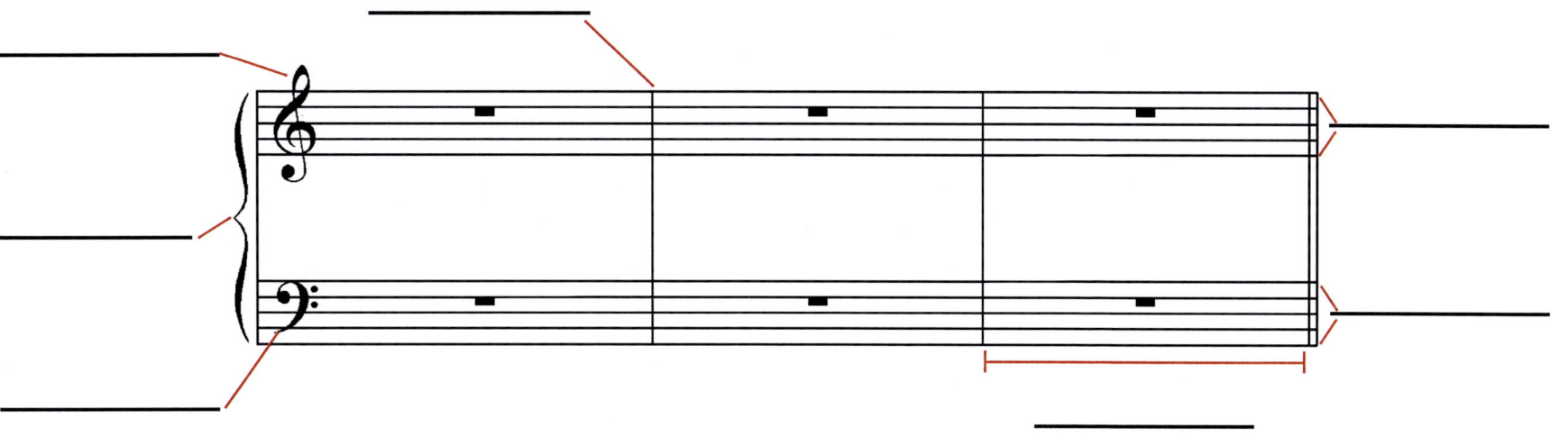

Grand Staff
Treble Clef
Bass Clef
Bar Line
Measure
Treble Staff
Bass Staff

Note Test

Name the note.

Certificate of Achievement

This certificate is presented to

_____

For achievement in completing
Piano Marvel Method
Level 1

_____ _____
Date   Signature